My Intimate Journey To Self

Lindsay ♡

My Intimate Journey To Self

An Indigo's story of
How to survive a transit period
and the surprise of a Soulmate

follow your heart.... ♡

Nancy Jo VanHook

Copyright © 2012 by Nancy Jo VanHook.

Library of Congress Control Number: 2012916618
ISBN: Hardcover   978-1-4797-1391-2
        Softcover   978-1-4797-1390-5
        Ebook   978-1-4797-1392-9

All rights reserved. No part of this book may be reproduced or transmitted in any form or by any means, electronic or mechanical, including photocopying, recording, or by any information storage and retrieval system, without permission in writing from the copyright owner.

This book was printed in the United States of America.

Rev. date: 04/03/2013

To order additional copies of this book, contact:
Xlibris Corporation
1-888-795-4274
www.Xlibris.com
Orders@Xlibris.com
109698

Contents

Chapter 1 Growing Up 13
Chapter 2 June 2010 36
Chapter 3 Rodolfo 56
Chapter 4 Theja 68
Chapter 5 Myself 85

Foreword

The Summer of 2010

That summer, I went out on my porch and noticed something awesome! I'm not even sure what drew me to go out that night. Maybe I was drawn by some enchantment I could not resist. I noticed the sun was about to set. I sat myself down in a wicker chair and gazed across the sky. The wind was blowing swiftly; I could smell rain. The orange sun with magenta hues sat, but there were these beautiful pink and purple clouds that hung above the sunset; then on top of that, there was a blanket of stars in the deep velvet blue sky. Then out of nowhere, I saw lightning, and thunder roared loudly with such power I got goose bumps! I wondered to myself how many people witnessed this phenomenon. I was so struck by this beauty; it was divine to behold such a sight, and I knew in that instant, something fantastic was about to happen to me!

I was frightened . . .

Prologue

Indigo . . .

I'm not that special, and I'm pretty ordinary when it comes to feelings and thoughts and how I do things. I'm just like everyone else out there. You know, like every other woman, I worry about my daughter first then the bills and the house and dinner and my hair and figure, and well, the list goes on and on and on, right? It's a vicious cycle every day—a routine that you are programmed to do once you become that woman who wants to keep up with the Joneses next door or just fit in to society, somehow . . .

Women worry about everything! I worry about all kinds of things, including how it is going to make a difference if I buy cage-free eggs or eat fresh vegetables versus frozen. Is donating money better, or is volunteering more helpful? I think both are needed, but where do I fit in? What is the bigger picture?

Then one day, I found myself in the most unwanted prison of my life! Myself. Yes, I was a prisoner in my own heart, body, mind, and soul. How do I fix what seems to be doing everything right and good and, well, perfect? Yes, I said perfect! My life made sense to me. I had everything—a house, a daughter, and even a husband and a job that was fulfilling. Not so fast, perfect, really? Then I went to a high school reunion and found out otherwise. I, all of a sudden, ran into a wall and began to rack my brains every day on it to figure out what happened to me. All of a sudden, my life made no sense anymore. I became confused and started to search. This was the beginning of a journey that I never thought could happen, least of all, me!

I work with disabled children every day, and I found my job to suit me well. I cared a lot about the children I worked with and wanted to do more and learn as much as I could about how to help them overcome their disabilities. Like I said, it was fulfilling to me! I didn't see these students as having a disability; I saw them as themselves. They were wonderful to me, and I liked them; I could imagine their situation . . .

I was only an aide at a school, but I thought I was okay. People often would tell me that I had a difficult job. They told me that I had patience and shook their heads in wonder. But I knew in my heart that these children were a miracle of God, and I had the honor to work with them. They were a side to God you often didn't get to see. I liked how they thought and worked with what God gave them. They were at times optimistic, and I knew I could learn something from them, so I was honored to meet them and learn from them.

I once worked with a boy that no one wanted to work with. He had a behavior problem. I heard all kinds of horror stories about him. One teacher told me that he would crawl under her desk and growl like a dog. Another told me that he would spit at you. He sounded more like an animal than a human. I heard enough, and I liked a challenge. But I'm sure he thought everyone else had a behavior problem.

I was introduced to this boy by the special education director. She walked me down the hallway where he was in the bathroom. The custodian close by told me that he was going to charge rent because he was always there. The director called his name and asked him to come out and meet Ms. Nancy, his new aide. Right away, he yelled out, "I hate all my aides!" He had an attitude, but I liked him already. I talked some more to the director about him, and she had pages and pages of many things that were wrong about him and only about a half page of what was good about him. Then she called for him again. He came out with these fat lenses for glasses and filthy, stinky coat that looked like a lawn mower ran over it. He could hardly see. His glasses were like the bottom of a Coke bottle. On his coat, there were bike track prints going across it; the pockets were hanging by threads, and the inside lining of the coat was becoming detached so you could see the white foam. But I think he liked the track marks on it. I smiled at him and introduced myself. He began to wash his hands and reminded me again that he hates all his aides. I told him that I totally got that. I told him I was glad for his honesty, and I hope he will always be honest with me because I liked that in a person.

He was staring at me through those thick round lenses for glasses. I told him, "Look, we can make this a bad thing or a good thing, but the choice is up to you." I was not going to force him to like me or do what I say. I see this as an opportunity for him if he would just listen and talk to me about what he wants and what he likes. I told him that I was a nice person, and I was willing to find things for him to earn for good behavior and get his work done.

I worked with other students before, and I understood charts and rewards. But he will have to work first, then I would be happy to let him have what he wants. He seemed interested; I then told him I could buy candy, snacks, or small toys. He said that he liked toys. I told him, "Great. Then I will buy toys!" The director then nodded at me and left down the hallway. We, however, walked to his classroom, and we talked to his teacher, and she agreed to the choices and began to put together a plan for his learning. It was good teamwork.

We had a wonderful relationship, and I grew very attached to him, and he became very popular with the other students and teachers. I'm not saying that everything went perfect, but things started to look up for him. I even bought him a new coat! That other one smelled so bad, and well, he was like a child of my own. I wanted him to be happy and cared for. I never knew I could be that way with someone else's child. It felt good to help.

There were a lot of students that I learned to care for, but when would I see that I too needed attention? There was a lot of love going out but nothing coming in for me . . .

I never took a second look at my life to think about me. I've always done what needs to be done for everyone. It was automatic for me to serve and help others. It is my nature, but I never thought about my own happiness. Really, I didn't. Okay, maybe a bit but never long enough to do anything about it. I always thought that I would retire at the school and become the nobody I was. I really thought that I was a nobody, and I was happy being a nobody. Am I making you sick yet?

Okay, I'll be honest with you. Inside my soul, I loved adventure, but from the outside, everyone depended on me to get the job done and to think of a way to help out with whatever need there was even if I did not get the credit for the idea. I often felt unappreciated and alone in my career. I always told myself, well, as long as the kids were being taken care of, then that was all that mattered. But later, this would all make me angry, and I would ask myself why I did not take the credit or go for any of my dreams. So at times, I would just daydream about "life."

I had worked as a model and did well at that too. I've been on TV commercials, newspaper ads, catalogs, runway shows, hair shows, conventions, promotions, billboards, and calendars. They used me for everything! They asked for me by name. I was dependable and friendly, and I had a very nice smile that everyone liked. Someone once told me that I reminded them of their first girlfriend, and then someone also told me that I looked like their sister or the girl-next-door type. I once was offered a chance to go to New York, but I put my family first and later regretted that I didn't go for that dream as well.

But this time, I needed to really sit myself down and take a look at my life. I needed to see my life pattern. So I started to write down my story to get a better look. I wanted to know where I got stuck so I could fix things. I needed to find out who I am again and where my strengths were and my weaknesses.

I'll get to the part you're really interested in, soon, but it's important that you know this about me first. But you see, there is more to tell you because this story gets really good. Just wait!

Chapter 1

Growing Up

When I was a youngster growing up, something happened to me that made me different, and I'll get to that part soon, I promise. But on the day I was born, January 9, 1963, I made an entrance into the world at about prime time TV hour. We lived in Florida at that time, and on that day, my dad was hit by a car on the way to the hospital. It was rush hour traffic; the man paid my dad five dollars for the damage. On a five dollar bill, there is Abraham Lincoln; right, this is an important part to the story, so remember this, okay? My dad tells this story all the time. The man in the car was black, not that this should matter, but it does, later. But no one really cared there was a baby girl born, but it was I, Nancy Jo VanHook.

Names are important, and my name is a variation of Anne, which means in Hebrew, "God has favored." Some think the name is also a variation of Grace, which means "God's favor." However, the name Nancy means kindness or a blessing, unconditional love, good will. My middle name "Jo" means the same, so I was a double blessing or kindness. The surname "VanHook" is an Americanized spelling for the Dutch surname "VanHoek." Antonie van Leeuwenhoek in 1764 invented the microscope and known as the "Father of Microbiology." Galileo also took credit for the invention, so I am in good company, and you will see how all this makes better sense and how a name really tells a lot about a person.

My parents really didn't know how to raise me. Most of the time, they would just shake their heads and wonder did that come out of me, or they would just accept it and own up to it and say, yeah, that is a part of me all right! I know what goes through a parent's mind; I mean I am a parent, but for the most part, they trusted God and just knew that God would show me the way. Are you getting my drift here? Yeah, they were strict Christians, and I was the youngest of three.

I had two older brothers who tormented me in my highchair. One would pull my hair, while the other, at the same time, would take my toy away. This is true; I have proof; I have pictures! Do I sound like every other youngest of the family? Yes, I got attention, the worst of it from two brothers. When puberty came along, good lord, I was in trouble! They like to poke and make fun of my developing breast and oversized trunk. I, all of a sudden, had; you think this might be funny, but I was not laughing!

I wanted to do everything my brothers were doing. If they were going to school, I wanted to go even if I was still in a crib. Isn't that human nature to want what you cannot have? Well, they would just stick their tongues out and laugh at me. I love my brothers, but they were only doing what brothers do best—torment; I had to become tough!

Brothers

There were times when my brothers did super nice things too. Like the time when Mom would put us on the couch to give us a spanking for something we did wrong. Isn't it funny how you don't remember what you did wrong, but you remember the spanking? That's why it is important to tell your kiddos why before the spanking. But you know, back then, things were different . . .

After sitting us down on the couch, Mom would go into the kitchen and pour herself a glass of Coke. She drank a lot of Coke; I could hear it fizz as she poured it over the ice, and we had to be quiet and wait for her. In the corner by the front door, there was a paddle for the spankings. It was made of wood. We all saw it every day, but it never came into mind until it was time for a spanking. Well, my oldest brother, Shawn, knew my mother's buttons well, and he could see the fear in our eyes about getting a spanking. We always did what Shawn said; he was smart, but he was the one that got us into trouble in the first place. He told me and my other brother, Bruce, to cry hard when she would spank us, and then she would not spank so hard.

Let me explain. I know my mom never intended to hurt us; this was how discipline was done when I was a child, and I'm not saying it is right or wrong. I'm just telling you the story, okay?

Well, Shawn went first and showed Bruce and I how to cry. Shawn would arch his back and yell "Ouch!" every time she would hit him. Mom said, "This hurts me more than you." I almost laughed because I knew it wasn't real. Shawn just showed us how to defuse pain. Well, we all gave a big, loud show of pain when she would spank, and it worked, and when mom left, we all laughed quietly to ourselves! I was ever so grateful for my Brother Shawn!

Then there was Bruce; he and I were close. I liked him. We could play for hours together. We knew how to share toys and naturally wanted to please each other. Not that we didn't fight! But it was still fun to fight with him. We would see just how far we could push each other before the other one would cry or go tell Mom.

I remember when Bruce would put both his knees on my elbows and my back to the floor, and he began to tap my forehead fast with his index finger and called it "Chinese water torture." I think he picked it up from TV somewhere. Then he would start to drool to intentionally put it on my face. Well, that was all I was going to take! I would have to kick him, and I knew where to kick! He got off fast. Only a sister could do this, you know. But it would all be over with fast, and then thirty minutes later, we would be playing together again with renewed respect.

There were other times too with being the opposite sex that we would be curious, but this is what it is like to be a brother and a sister. We are different sex, and that is too intriguing, isn't it?

Okay, here it goes . . . I was young and started to go through puberty. Boys are curious, girls are too, but I think boys are more so. I remember when I would take a bath. I could play for hours in the tub. The door to the bathroom had this large crack in it where the door closed at the bottom. The more I think about it, I believe that my brothers made it like that! Well, I was careful and put a small towel in it just to make sure no one could see in. Then when I was getting out of the bath, I noticed that the towel was down, and the crack was exposed. I stuck the towel back in. Then while I was drying off, the towel tumbled down again. One of my brothers had a wire hanger and was poking at the towel to get it down. I knew what was going on; it was my brothers looking in on me! I yelled at the top of my lungs. "Mom! Shawn and Bruce are looking in on me!" I heard the running of feet and snickering. Well, the bathroom got a new door.

You know, my brothers have always been there, and Bruce has given me a hug or two if I needed it. I just was not very good at asking for them. Growing up can be hard sometimes, and it's nice to have your brothers. Bruce could often help me see myself. He once told me that I was a giver and not a taker, and this would one day get me in trouble. I always remembered that, and I wish I could change that, but I love to help and give from the heart, but I can stand up for myself if I have to, and my brothers taught me that.

My brothers were important to me, and Shawn got a lot of my parent's attention, and Bruce needed help in school, and they took the attention off me. My mother once told me that I was always very good at doing everything for myself. Mom said she never worried about me.

I too worried about my brothers and took on that role of nurturing and applied it in all of my life. I worried about my brothers. I looked out for them when I could. It was my nature to be their sister. But I did not like my role, I did not want to lead, I felt it was Shawn's role, but he was not able to. Bruce was nurturing toward me but still unable to be a serious role model, I thought. I had the role to be a good example for what is right and good. Shawn was a class clown, and Bruce was shy at times, but the older he got, the better he was able to assert himself. I always felt I had to be good for my parents. Not that my brothers are not good, but I felt this burden to prove something.

But God has a plan. Do you like how I am setting this up? Yes, God has a plan. Wait till you hear this; you won't believe this!

Family Ties

Every family has their traits, and in my family, there are some things that have happened that are common and uncommon. Now you need to pay attention because this part of the story is important too. I never heard this story until later in life. My mother, Joann, had this experience when she was a young girl after her brother, Tom, got hurt one day. Mom was older, about five or six years old. Tom was still a toddler. He was outside playing, and this was when my mother's real dad was in the Second World War, so he was gone. Well, back to the story. My uncle was outside, and then these boys were walking down the street and threw this glass milk jug to the ground. Well, a fairly large piece of glass got in Tom's eye. Their mom, my grandma, Ruth, had to take him to the doctor. So my mother, Joann, had to stay at her great-grandma's house. She then dragged my mom to church to pray for my Uncle Tom.

My mom had never been to church; her mother just didn't go, so this was Mom's first experience at church. Mom said that when they started to pray, they began to beat the pews, walls, and each other. Yelling hallelujah and praise the Lord! They wailed and moaned; it had to be something to see. My mother was frightened by all this commotion. Well, that is how they pray; that is how they help the person they are praying for in this church. Have you ever heard about the "holy rollers?" My mom says she has never seen anything like it, ever, still today! That was my mother's first spiritual experience.

My uncle got the glass out of his eye, and the doctor said that he might not be able to see out of it. That was not the case for my uncle. He got better, and he sees just fine out of both eyes. I guess the prayers worked! My mother's eyes were opened to a new world as well; she began to seek out more spiritual experiences, and that is how she ended up with my father. My father always attends church every Sunday, every week of his life, no matter what—rain, snow, the apocalypse—he always goes. They started dating, and my father took her to church. My mother liked this.

Then my uncle had this experience when he was in the air force. By this time, my uncle was a bad boy. He was an angry young man, got into a lot of fights, drank and cursed, smoked, and well, he had a lot to figure out. His dad left him, my mother, and my grandma for some other women; and he was still angry about these things.

Then one day, my uncle wanted to do something very wrong. He was on his way to do it, his mind already made up. And just as he was about to do it, he got this really bad feeling that he had something mean and nasty behind him. "It was the devil!" My uncle said and looked with his eyes wide open and voice so wobbly. He got so scared that he did not do that horrible thing. He knew then that he had to change the way he was living and not that he went straight to church. He just cleaned up his life more. He has been married four times and has children in two different countries. But he did find his angel, Barb, and she has been his beacon of light.

I know you are wondering what he wanted to do that was so bad, but that is not important. What is important is that he did not do it. You could say Tom got the glass out of his eye again, and he understands the story of "Little Red Riding Hood" profoundly. I noticed that he collects these unusual Red Riding Hoods glass figures. God works in mysterious ways!

Grandfather (Chet)

Now, my story . . . I want to tell you about my grandfather. He was my dad's father, and he had Native American in his heritage. There was a story that was told in the family about the Indians that kidnapped some family members and how these family members lived with the Indians. Well, adventitiously, these family members got away. But that is all I know about the story. But this is important to know this about my grandfather; you will see why later.

My grandfather moved in with us when my grandmother died. Her name was Bertha. He lived in Florida, but we moved him in with us so he would not be alone. We lived in Missouri at this time. He loved my grandmother so much. He missed her. He was so sad when he moved in. This is an important part to my story because it had an impact on our family. He wept in silence for her; he had us to love, but he missed his mate. It was hard to take every day to see him long or yearn for her. I wanted to console him as a child. So I hugged him many times, and I would try to make him laugh or smile. It made me feel better to have him happy. I didn't want him to be sad anymore. I loved my grandfather a lot. It would make me sad to see him brokenhearted. Can you see why this is an important part to the story?

When he moved in, it was nice to have him around. I liked it a lot. I remembered when my mother would baby sit a little girl, and she would go up to my grandfather and have him rub her back. I got jealous and put a stop to that! I pushed her out of the way and then got where she was so he could rub my back instead. My grandfather laughed! I did not want to share my grandpa with her. He was my grandpa, and he was going to rub my back, not hers! I managed to put a smile on his face. I knew he loved me, and I often wondered about him because he was a quiet man. He hardly said a word around us. But he was the kindest, gentlest man I knew at the time besides my dad. He always made time to be with us, but this I can and will remember. He bought each one of his grandchildren a Bible with our names on it. I still have it to this day.

Well, my grandfather had emphysema from smoking too much when he was younger. However, it all caught up to him one day. When my family was outside riding horses, I came in to go to the bathroom and found my grandfather with his oxygen on, like so many times before. I could hear it very well; I hear it today when I think about it. I went to go look in on him, and here is where it gets weird. Are you ready because I wasn't!

My grandfather had his head back in his chair, eyes closed. I went to touch him; this is the part that changed my life forever. When I touched him, I realized he was dead; he had that lifeless feel to him but still warm. Then I saw this Indian from the corner of my eye on my grandfather's bed with drum music. It also could have been the sound of a heartbeat, now that I think about it. However, I quickly pulled away and ran outside to tell my mother. I quickly thought not to tell her about the Indian. I just told her that grandfather was dead; this was more important—see how my life is changing already . . .

Then my mother calls us in to sit on the couch and waits for the ambulance to arrive. It's a day that never escapes my mind. I then became very interested in Indians, and it has been a secret all my life, but this will all make better sense later. Later, you will see how God places things in your life to give you a map for the really hard times to come. I was about nine then, in the third grade, but this was only one event that started another. You'll see how all this will make sense later . . .

But I got a gift that day, and it was the Indian.

My dad believes that my grandpa had died of a broken heart because he missed my grandma. He only lived with us for about four or five years, but I was the one that was there for him when he died. He was not alone. I was there for him and I missed him greatly . . .

Mother (Joann)

My mother . . . I love my mother. I can safely say that most of us love our mothers! My mother is a saint! She really is; she is always out there helping with whatever project there is to help the needy or sick, and she got us kids to help along with them. We were always making something—blankets for a nursing home or stuffed toy for a hospital. This is noble, right? My mom is awesome.

We use to bake and decorate cookies at Christmas and sell them. Everyone wanted them! It became a big business. Mom had us busy, and we just did what she wanted. It was fun to do, and we got to talk and visit, and everyone knew what their job was. The cookies were from a sugar cookie recipe, and we iced and decorated them with cake decorating tubs. We made Santa, snowmen, Christmas trees, Rudolph, bells, and ginger bread, men and women. My mom was known all over in the school district.

She kept us busy with crafts like homemade potholders for Christmas, and she taught us how to be thankful for all the wonderful things we had. My mom grew up poor, so she knew what it was like to be without. She taught us to be creative and make things with what you have.

But there was a mischievous side to her too that I liked. Well, she always had a reason for her behavior too. My mother liked to take things that are not hers. She once dug up a neighbor's flowers, and my Brother Shawn was there to help. Mom simply said that the flowers were on the road and anyone could have them, and they were wild flowers too. You see, that sounded like a good reason to a youngster. She would also take those sugars and salts that were there at restaurants. I mean one or two was enough, right? No, my mom took a small purse full!

She was still a saint to me, and to all the people at church and anyone that knew her knew they could count on my mom to give and give of her heart and soul to any cause to any purpose. I love her for that, and I know she loves me too.

But I wanted her to give me attention sometimes. Shawn was better at getting her attention. I just got left out, I felt, and there just had to be something wrong with me, right? I became very attached to my Brother Bruce. We could play for hours and enjoyed the bond. See how a family works together.

Shawn is that one in the family that had the attention because of his behavior. He could be bizarre at times. I think he had ADHD as a child, and my parents hadn't had clue how to help him. I know this now because I work with children like this every day. Shawn had no focus, and my parents spent all their lives trying to "fix" Shawn. I even wanted to help, but I always thought Shawn was doing a great job getting exactly what he wanted—his parents' attention. Shawn was happy; he was smart and knew how talk to anyone. He was popular in school and kept himself busy all the time.

I remember the time when Mom left us youngsters out in the car while she went in to do something for a friend of hers. She was not gone long, but it was just long enough for Shawn to do something crazy. Shawn decided to put the car in gear while we were in it, and the car started to roll backward! Well, Mom came out just in time to find the car rolling. She began to scream at us to open the door! Shawn opened the door, and Mom stopped the car. Everybody has someone like this in their family, right? You just learn your place in the family and work independently.

Bruce was there for me, and I knew it. He thinks I was there for him, but he helped me through some tough times when I was growing up. Bruce was fun and caring, and we shared a mutual affection for each other as brother and sister. However, I was talking about my mother, right? Well, I guess we all came out of her, so I'm giving you a good look at her.

Dad (Tom)

Well, here it goes, the one person I have the hardest time talking about. Yes, I used to be afraid of him. At times, I hated him; I don't know why. Maybe that is because we are so much alike. I see in him what I dislike about myself, and that is hard to take. I know that he cares a great deal about us kids, but sometimes he needs to back off and just let us grow on our own, but I understand that he was only trying to be a good parent.

It's hard to know when to stay out of your kid's life. I know that he had an idea about what he wanted for us because he did such a good job with us, but there is free will, and growing up means you are going to make mistakes, and it is hard to watch your kids make mistakes and learn from them. Especially if one of your kiddos is hardheaded like me. I too liked to be right; I hate being wrong. I was always sure I was right because I could think and solve my way through some difficult situations. I mean after all my dad taught me how to do this, right? He should trust me. I too am from him, and he should have confidence in his children. But he was not always that way. He felt the need to protect us.

He likes to teach a lesson, but he never stops talking about this lesson. I have to get up and leave because he is driving a point over and over again. One day, I told him to stop doing this and that it was making it hard for me to come out to see him. My dad wants to teach a bible lesson every time I go out to his house. I just wanted to talk about a movie or my day at work or something else, but not my dad. He wanted to make sure I still remembered God in my life. I hated him for it; I hated God for it. Then finally, I told him to stop, and he respected my wish. Now, I remind my dad often that I remember what he has taught me. But my dad can make a remark that can cut to the bone. His honesty can hurt, and I know today that I got that from him. His honesty or his need to be right at times has caused me to be somewhat rebellious. But he makes me so angry! So I learned tactfulness and tried to use it as much as possible.

My dad also likes to be outdoors. He loves to be in nature, and he can tell you the names or every tree, bush, and plant out there. If he didn't know, then he would find out. He would know everything about them and what their purpose was. I was amazed with his knowledge.

He took us blackberry hunting in the summer. First, we would get dressed in long sleeves and pants. Then Dad would spray us down with bug spray. After that, Dad would take us through tall grass and into the woods and teach us about the bugs and their use in nature. He knew about spiders and snakes, and well, he taught us that there was a balance, and we should respect that. Then finally, we would find the blackberries, and we ate them as we picked them. It was a nice treat! We filled our buckets and went home, and Mom made a blackberry cobbler, and it was delicious . . .

My dad is also a proud marine. He served his country, and he has a tattoo with his name on his arm. I remember when I would look at it as a little girl. I would point at it and wonder about it. My dad said that he got it on his arm so if he was found dead, then they could identify him and send him home to his mother. When I got older, the story would change a bit. He told me that it was the stupidest thing he ever did, my dad, always trying to teach a lesson.

I guess now you know that I was a very impressionable child. Now, I will tell you about what my father said. My dad likes to think, and he also likes to be right about what he knows, so he reads a lot. One time, he started a conversation in the car coming home from church. This had to be about what the minister was preaching about, but I was not paying attention that day. You know, I was just a little kid, probably playing in the seat with crayons and a pad of paper. Well, he had this story to tell all of us, and I remember it well.

He started the story with all of us in the ocean and drowning. My dad asked whom he would save first. I was perplexed. It was a complicated question, I thought. I was baffled to even ponder the solution. All of us kids thought hard, and drowning is not a good way to die. Well, my dad said he would save my mother first. My dad did not tell us why he would save her first. He only wanted us to think about that answer.

Well, much later in the day, I asked my dad why he would save my mother first. I had to know why, and then I could better understand and come up with a solution. His answer was that she was his other half and couldn't lose her. So my survival instincts kicked in, and I told my father I needed to learn how to swim. He was happy with whatever answer I gave him that day because I was thinking, but he was teaching me to use many levels of thought that day. If you are alone, you need to learn how to survive, then you can help others like your brothers. And then there is the will to live to consider, and I had a strong will to live, and Dad said that asking for help is okay but first try it on your own. Dad said if he saved our mother, then we would have a better chance in life, and a mother is important to a child, and he loved her so much. He knew my mother would make sure we were okay. My dad was the voice of reason, but he also had his heart connected with his thought. I admired him.

The Farm

Here's the last event in my childhood I'll tell you about. This happened within the same year. Are you ready for this? Okay, I thought we had a wonderful childhood when it came to my dad and my mom and how they provided for us. We had a farm with a cow for fresh milk, dogs, cats, and chickens for fresh eggs, sheep, and steers for fresh meat. We also had a garden for fresh vegetables and fruit trees. We had it good; it was like *Little House on the Prairie!* We were always busy and liked it a lot there on the farm.

But we also had horses. These animals are big and beautiful and needed care every day just like all the other animals on the farm. Every day, you have to clean their stall, brush them, clean their feet, and ride them. We did all this. We would trail ride our horses with the neighbors. It was fun. We took them to horse shows. We were in the 4-H club. Any child would love a life like this! There are so many stories to share with you about my life on this farm, but this story sticks out the most. Okay, I'll get to the part you've been waiting for.

Horses

Let me first introduce you to our horses. I remember my mom's horse. She was a dappled tan, almost white mare. Her name was Nosy; she was a fox trotter, and she would get spooked about everything, but my mom could handle her. Nosy would move sideways to avoid something she did not like or was suspicious of, but mom would just put her hand on her big neck to calm Nosy down. Nosy would breathe real hard through her nose and stare at whatever was spooking her.

My dad had this big beautiful black walking horse. His mane and tail had silver in it. His name was Rascal. He was spirited and fast and held his head high, and his eyes looked crazy, spirited, but he was magnificent to look at.

Shawn had a chubby quarter horse palomino. She was short, sweet, and gentle, and her name was Cinnamon.

Bruce had an Indian horse or paint. She was cute and had dark brown and white patches and so sweet. Her name was Cindy.

My horse was a very large appaloosa, also an Indian horse. He was a gentle giant, and nothing frightens him. He was calm. I loved him so much! His name was Smokey.

Now, I can get on with the part of the story you want to hear. Believe me, it's not a happy part of the story, but it had a very large impact on my life, and horses will play a big part in it.

The Accident

One day, my parents and, brother, Shawn went out for a ride on their horses. Bruce and I had to stay home and weed the garden. I'm not sure, but I think it was because we got in trouble for something, and Shawn somehow escaped the punishment. However, they left, and Bruce and I got busy to clean the garden of weeds. Then all of a sudden, we heard the running hoofs of horses. They got closer, and then we saw Nosy first, and then five minutes later, we saw my dad's horse, Rascal, with no one on them, running fast through the yard to the barn.

This is an image that never escapes my mind. It is still there today, vividly! This was not a good sign. I began to panic. A neighbor came in the garden with Bruce and me. This is an important part to the story again. This neighbor was the one that helped us get the horses back in the barn and in their stalls. He was a black man, and he was so nice to Bruce and me. This had an important influence on me—one of trust and kindness. Shawn came back on his horse, Cinnamon, and helped too, but I ran up the road to see what had happen, by myself.

I found Mom on the road with my dad holding her in his arms talking to Mom. She was not responding to my dad. I kept running toward them.

Then Dad saw me and yelled to me, "Nancy, stop, go home, and help your brothers. The ambulance is coming!" I didn't want to leave, but I was obedient and left as my father had told me. It was the longest moments in my life! Then finally, the ambulance came, and I watched as they put her and my father in the ambulance. They left, and my mind is blank. I'm not sure why it is blank, but it still is.

Chaos

The next thing I remember is when we went to church, and everyone was hugging us. I didn't know what had happen to my mother; I was waiting to hear from her, but no one said anything to us. I don't remember crying or anything like that; I am only confused about what was going on. Then finally, Dad took us kids to the hospital. This is a good sign, right? Mom must be alive! I was happy to go and see my mother, but we were not allowed to see her. We had to sit outside the room and wait. We did this many times with my dad, and many friends came and sat with us. We also stayed at a neighbor's house, the Tutterow's. Then finally, Grandma came and got us and took us home.

There was a lot of family and church people there. My mom was in the hospital for twenty-eight days, and in those twenty-eight days, we went through a lot. There was family and church people and food being brought in every day for us. Everyone was so nice and helpful; they even cleaned the house and did our laundry. I never saw anything like it! What a blessing to have so many nice people.

Then finally, we were allowed to go see my mother at the hospital. I remember her in the bed with tubes in her arms and an oxygen mask on her face. She was smiling at us, but we were not allowed to touch her. She was still very sick. There were doctors and nurses coming in and out checking in on her, taking her blood pressure, and taking her blood and temperature, and well, I was confused about a lot. What happen, and why isn't anyone telling us? Why isn't Shawn talking about this? He was there when it happened. Did I ask him? Did he tell anyone else? I don't remember anything like that; only I didn't know, and I wanted my mother home and back to normal. I needed her!

I remember that time I ended up in the principal's office at school. Yeah, I hit a girl in the face. She said some bad things about my mother. It made me furious, so I hit her, and she fell to the ground with a thud. She cried. It was recess. She was saying I was a baby, and my mother wasn't sick at all. No one talks about my mother in a bad way! My mom was in the hospital, sick! She was not a very nice little girl. I was getting too much attention at school, I guess, so she was jealous of that. She wanted to hurt me or start a fight. Well, I showed her a thing or two about manners. How dare her!

The teacher dragged me to the office. She told me that she was disappointed in me. Mrs. Shots had this very bright red lipstick; I can still remember it. They called home, I got a spanking, and I remembered to cry hard. So I got written up and sent home. I just created more trouble for my dad, but I was right, and I was sure of it. They needed to hear my side of the story.

This was all chaos to a nine-year-old!

Home

It wasn't until Mom came home in a wheel chair that we got the story of what had happened. This is the part that was both beautiful and sad to me. Make sure you pay attention to how my mom tells the story; it was important that we heard it from her, she said. It had a great influence on us! I remember my mother was in the bedroom and then invited us in by ourselves with just her there to tell the story.

She smiled and waved us into the room then told us that Nosy had fell on her and crushed her insides, and she almost died, but Dad had gotten her to the hospital just in time to fix her up. She described herself as Humpty Dumpty and how the doctors put her back together again with a smile. She then began to tell us all the details of what had happen from start to finish. Mom told the story of Nosy getting spooked about something in the bushes and reminded us how Nosy was and how she tried to calm her down. Mom said that this time, she had no control for some reason. Mom has put her hand on Nosy's neck, but this time, it did not work.

If you can keep the head down on a horse, then this prevents the horse from rearing, and Nosy reared out of fear and fell backward on my mother. My mom was riding with a western saddle, and Nosy landed on Mom and rolled on her to get up. I'm not sure how many of you know about horses, but they are big animals, and a western saddle has a horn on it! No one could do anything to help. "It was a freak accident," Mom said.

Mom then processed to tell us about her loss, she had lost six inches of small intestine, parts of her stomach, large intestine, and liver. She lost her spleen all together. She had crushed ribs and broke her arm and leg. She had internal bleeding and nearly died. "It was by the grace of God that I am alive," Mom said. Then Mom took her robe off to see her body lying on the bed so we could see her very large scar. She pointed to it and showed us where it started and where it ended. The scar ran from her heart to her private area. I think I was more shocked to see my mother's body than the scar! She had on a bra and panties, but my mother was a beautiful woman, and she had a nice body back then, but now she has a scar on it. This will never go away on her body or in the minds of her children. But all of this has an important part to play in my life, and I will get to it soon, and it will all make total sense, later. But my mother is a living miracle . . .

Mom did, however, get back on top of Nosy and rode her, once. For some reason, it was to prove something to herself that she was not afraid of the horse that nearly killed her. We did not put the horse to sleep or shoot it. Instead, Mom and Dad had her bred to have a baby. This helped Nosy, and we kids loved watching the baby colt being born and raised by her mother.

Grandpa (Francis)

Okay, deep breath . . . Now I must tell you about my other grandpa. He was a retired army drill sergeant, and he was not my mom's natural father. He drank and cursed sometimes, but my mother asked him to not do that around us kids, and he respected her wish. He was pretty quiet around us, and he once made an impression on me.

One time when my brothers and I were playing in the laundry room, I stepped on top of this cooler and broke the lid. It was one of those cheap Styrofoam coolers. I felt bad about that but quickly forgot about it.

Then my grandpa pulled me and my brothers into the room together and asked us what had happened, and he reminded us that it was more important to tell the truth because he hated a liar. And believe me, no one wanted to make my grandpa angry. It was harsh punishment. He would drag you by the ear and make you do something! My dad said that was why my uncle had ears that stuck out funny because he got his ears pulled so much by Grandpa. He would make you pick up toys and untie your shoes at the front door. You don't just slip them off, and it was not your mother's job to do—it was yours. Now, he never hurt any of his grandchildren, but my mother told me many stories about him, and I had a genuine fear for my grandpa or Francis. He was my mother's stepdad, but she had respect for him, and so did I.

Okay, back to the story about the cooler. He looked all of us in the face, and we all looked at each other as if to telecommunicate and remember we were little at this time. What was the punishment for the crime? What if I lie, and then he finds out? There was a lot to consider. I then told grandpa that I broke the lid, and I was sorry. He took a deep breath and put his hand on my arm and told me that he was proud of me for telling the truth. He said he was going to go easy on me. He asked me to help him clean up the mess, and then I could go back and play. He then reminded me again that it is always better to be honest and not to ever tell a lie. I was so thrilled to make my grandpa happy that day! This lesson has stuck with me always, and I had a good time helping my grandpa clean up the mess. I liked him a lot.

Now, my mother's side of the family was the loud, talkative, smiling, hugging, and kissing type of people. They had lots of fun every time they got together! I could really tell you some stories about them. I laughed so hard when they were around!

My dad's side of the family were often more reserved and spiritual. There was order, and things were comfortable, relaxed, and nurturing. There was always a good reason for everything around them. They helped you learn about the world around you. I liked that too. It was fun growing up in my family, and I had a wonderful childhood because of all of them; thanks to God.

Grandma (Ruth)

Okay, one other thing before I get to the part you've been waiting for. I had a grandma, and I became really close with her the older I got, as an adult. She moved in with us after my grandfather Francis died. She missed him a lot, but we had family gatherings, and she played an important part in all of them. I miss her now that I'm talking about her again. She was so much fun to be around, and she loved her sisters, and whenever they would get together, they were loud and joked around, and there was always good food too. Everyone loved her, and she could talk with anyone. My dad always said that no one was ever a stranger to her. Grandma could talk to anyone about anything. I believe I got that from her.

My grandma had what she called a "peg leg"; it was an artificial or prosthetic leg when I knew her. She lost it to bone cancer when she was a young lady. She did not have a prosthetic leg until she got married the second time. She either had crutches or that "peg leg," but she got around well. Nothing stopped her. Grandma liked to be in the mix of everything and in everyone's business. She always had a wonderful grin or smile. Her eyes were bright and happy, and I loved her so much.

Well, one day in January the night before my birthday, she would always call or send a card in the mail. I loved that about her; she thought always of her family. This time, however, I got my card two weeks before my birthday. I was surprised, so I called her the night before my birthday. I don't know why, but I had heard from my mother that she was feeling down and ill, so I wanted to call her and thank her for the card. I really wanted to go out to visit her, and I often did, but it was late, and I was thinking about her a lot, so I called. She picked up the phone and told me that she was thinking about me when I called. This happened a lot between us, and she would always talk with me about things like this. It made me feel good because she shared with me her feelings and thoughts and experiences about the psychic realms. We enjoyed little talks like that; I know I did. I would listen to every word she said. Grandma and I had a special connection, and I felt the need to comfort her, so we talked for a long time about everything—the past and the present. She always told me that she could remember my birthday because President Nixon and I shared the same one. She always reminded me of that. Why was that important to her, I don't know, but it made her happy, and if grandma was happy about it, I was pleased. Then I wished her a good evening, and I told her I would pray for her to get better, and I told her that I loved her then hung up.

That next day, my mother called and told me that my grandma had died on the couch, on my birthday. I was so very sad and confused about why she would die on my birthday, but I had to think. Well, she gave me a gift; it will be a good way to remember her. I will never forget about her. She made an impression on me this way; I believe she wanted that connection to me, and I still have her when I need her. She is there to guide me with many things. I know the connection is on who I can trust; she has her own way of telling me. I'm sure other people have a connection like this with someone special. I cannot be the only one like this.

Shit!

Okay, that is a bad word, right? But this word, along with some other words, really defines a feeling or a situation. Profanity can be used to get a point across when you are upset, discouraged.

I learned about discouragement... This comes along with relationships, careers, and parenting. This is when you need your faith the most. Because you really want to give up, but you need to find what you really want or define better what you really need. Look around and say "shit" when you have to. You feel better! Then you can calm down and be more focused. Yes, there are consequences to saying these words depending on where you work and who you are with. These words stir, surprise, and confuse feelings in people. Many recognize your pain, and others hate you. You learn who your friends are.

I have a long history of relatives that use profanity. I'm not proud of this. I'm only stating the facts. I had an Aunt Betty. She was good with using these words but not around us kids. My mother made sure her aunts and family did not use it round us, but sometimes Aunt Betty could not help it. It was her way of speech. She smoked and talked with a cigarette moving up and down in her mouth. She even had the most fascinating cigarette lighter. It was a pistol, and every time she would grab her pistol lighter, I just had to look and watch her! She would pull the trigger, and a flame was there on the end, and she would light her cigarette. For a child, this was captivating! Aunt Betty was very thin and walked with a jerk, and her eyes often bulged while she looked at you. She was sort of attractive but had this boyish charm to her. She dressed nice, and her hair was dark. I loved her very much because she was interesting and funny to me. She could make me smile!

Well, back to the story . . . My dad had moved us kids out to the boonies. Why? Well, my brother got caught smoking a cigar with one of the neighbors. The neighborhood children became a little too influential, for my dad, so we moved out on more acres and brought the whole farm with us. We were far away from people now. But it was nice, and my dad built a log cabin on the new piece of land. We had everything a child could want. Fruit trees, vegetable gardens, animals, and the stars at night, and it was peaceful.

Well, when I was a girl, I heard this word "shit" come from a surprising person to me. But it taught me that we have to pop, and using a bad word sometimes just describes your feelings of discouragement. It puts things into prospective. Sometimes there's no other way to say it!

One time when I was a girl, there was a flood in the sheep barn. The barn was made of metal. It was one of those very nice ones with the sliding doors and pens inside. My dad always got the best of everything. However, it snowed a lot that winter, and the snow was melting and on the side of the barn door entrance where the sheep went in for the night. The land next to the barn was higher, but it was not a problem until that spring. The barn was flooded on one end, and Dad said we needed to clean it up because the sheep were getting ready to lamb and needed a dry place to sleep.

So we spent the whole day there—my dad, my mom, and my brothers and I—cleaning the barn. It was stinky, and everyone had on their cover alls and got very dirty. But no one complained; we did our work. We wanted to help the sheep. It was important for them to have a dry and clean place for them to sleep. It was not a nice job!

But on the way out of the barn with a bucket of manure, there was no other way to do it. We could not shovel it on to a truck. It had to be moved with buckets! Well, my mom tripped, and the bucket of liquid manure hit the ground and went up into the air, and some of it hit my mom in the face. She said, "Shit!" My dad said, "Now, Joann, don't talk like that." My mom said, "Well, it is shit, and we are in deep shit!" That was it! We were all in shit, and no one liked it one bit. So Mom just defined the moment. My mother's side of the family was notorious for swearing, but I was a bit surprised. Mom was just discouraged and tired and went back to her roots

My brothers and I started to giggle, and my mother, with a half grin, pulled her gloves off, took out a hankie from inside her coveralls, and wiped her face off. We all felt better. We got right back to work with a smile and finished it, and the sheep had a dry place to sleep now. There was fresh straw down, and it looked clean and nice. My dad the next day fixed the door with a bobcat and leveled the ground outside. It was all fixed. Now, that was a good example for proper use of profanity.

Process of Being

How many lives does one live on Earth? Is Earth the only planet with life, our Universe the only Universe? No one knows for sure . . .

If one is born as human on Earth and then soul dies but body lives, changes, and then becomes a new soul but the same, is that possible? You can then remember your past and learn from mistake. This is growth because the mind is still in the same body.

Chapter 2

June 2010

Class Reunion, Gerry

Now, let me get to the present day. Now this is the part you will just shake your head and wonder about me because it's not who I am. Remember I told you that I went to a class reunion. It was a high school reunion. I'm getting sick to my stomach already. Well, I met him at the restaurant, like he asked. I started to think about him a lot. He contacted me through a classmate's Web site. He was always so smart, and I knew he would make something of himself, and he did! He was very successful. He is an engineer at a very large company. He has a very nice job.

Gerry was living his dream. I admired him so much for his hard work, and I always knew he would go far; I just knew he would. I was a bit intimidated by him, but I made my way over to him when he waved me down. I saw him over there finally, but he was off by himself with his family. He brought his wife and kids! I was all by myself; I tried to get my partner to go with me, but he did not want to meet my high school classmates, so I invited my friend, and she did not show up. I was alone.

I went over there, and I remember how he could make me feel. He could still make me feel that way . . . He had a power over me, and he knew it! My eyes stuck to his face with a trancelike zombie walk over to him. I was pathetic. I could not help myself. I felt his eyes stare right through me. Am I not pathetic? He was the one. He was my soul mate, and I could not have him, but he had a plan. Why else was he here tonight? So there I was in front of the man that I loved. What was I going to do now? So I did what any friend would do when meeting their friends again. I leaned over and gave him a kiss, on the cheek, and then smiled at him and said, "Gerry, I'm so happy to see you again after all these years! How are you?" Was I too much? Did I do the right thing? I think I was handling it great considering the situation.

He then asked me to sit down, with me sitting closer to him and across his wife. I decided to just stand where I was and began to shake hands with his wife and kids as I introduced myself as Gerry's friend from high school. Gerry told me that his wife knew about us as a couple in high school, so it was awkward for me, but I tried to stay calm. I liked everyone and smiled at each of them to try and relax myself, and them. His daughter told me that she liked my earrings. Well, I thought that was nice, so I smiled back at her and thanked her and then began to find something I liked about her. I did and I told her that I liked her shirt. I then noticed that Gerry's son had something that I recognized from working with disabled children. I was surprised to see this. I wanted to offer my opinion but didn't. It wasn't the right moment yet.

Then I pulled out a picture of my family. I didn't want to tell him that my partner and I were separated. It was only casual talk at this point. Well, he stared at the photo. He even got out his glasses to get a better look, I thought. He is wondering about my partner and my daughter. He was trying to make sense of it all. I knew he would not be able to. I gave up a long time ago why our relationship broke up. What the hell happened with this made-in-heaven-soul-mate relationship? And how did we end up with other partners?

Oh, please let's not go there now! So I took back the photo and put it away. I had a nice conversation with everyone and then decided to go. I felt uncomfortable and wanted to leave at this point. His wife looked so much like I did when we were dating, and she was younger than him. So I left, and this was only the beginning of a journey that started a revolution inside myself.

I then went home after being with my other classmates and visiting for a while. When I got up the next day, I checked my e-mail, and there was a message from Gerry. He told me how wonderful it was to see me and that I looked beautiful. I melted and wanted so much to talk with him. Instead, I e-mailed him back and told him the same. I wanted to catch up on what was going on with him, and I even sent him some old photos of us when we were dating as kids in high school. Gerry would send me YouTube of music videos. I loved that! It was a long correspondence affair through e-mail, and I was becoming attached to him emotionally. He would send out invitations in a way to come and see him, but I could not do it. I still had this honor of mine to keep. I was still married, and he was married.

I was honest and told him about my marriage and how I was separated from my partner and wanted to get out from that. I then asked him about his marriage, finally, and he told me that he had a "strong" marriage. What? Then why the meeting? Why the e-mails? why? I had to work this through, but he was not responding to me in this way, so I cut it off. He was telling a lie! He wanted me, but he still wanted his family whole, and I respect that, but I could not have an affair! I even one day sent him a sorry, an apology, but he didn't get it. He didn't understand why I was saying sorry. I was sorry I let him go a long time ago, and I wanted to have him again, but it was not going to work out.

Now I know a lot of women get themselves into relationships like this, and they are hard to get out of. I did, and it *hurt* me to do it. And let me tell you; I *cried*! I cried loud and hard, and I got attention! Wait till you hear about this; you won't believe this! Does this part of the story sound familiar?

I started to down load YouTube to my Facebook wall. I could not talk to anyone about my emotional affair with the heart. I was in pain; I felt as if I could not deal with my heartbreak. There was only one thing to do—download music and movies that had a meaning to how I was feeling. It was like scrape booking for my emotions.

Anyway, Facebook was cold with only words. No one can see how you feel; no one can really hug you and tell you, "It's going to be all right; you can deal with this." I needed space to mourn my loss, and I did it on Facebook, big time! I was puking my guts out, emotionally. I only had like ten friends at the time, so I thought it would be okay. No one really cares, right? I mean my friends put up with me, but they didn't know how to handle me, so they just allowed me to cry and puke. Thanks guys!

No one is watching me do this. I tried to go to a counselor, and I talked to her about it, but I was in so much pain. I was in so much pain. I started the YouTube with an Indian story, *The Indian in the Cupboard* then followed by *Phantom of the Opera, Remember Me,* and *Hachiko.* Then the *Horses* began to come in as well, the fast running horses like *Sea Biscuit.* I was on a roll. Does any of this resemble anything familiar to you?

I was stressed and the Indian, I believed, was my guide, but I had not even tried to talk to him, ever, but I needed him now. I always knew in a way that he was a spirit guide but simply could not handle being different. I always wanted to be like everyone else. I was raised to believe in God, and this was going against everything I knew to be right or normal, and I wanted to be normal! But I was in so much pain that I called for his help.

I always ignored my pain, and others came before me, but this was so hard to ignore. The past came back and in my face like a ghost; I had to do something. I began to do what my ghost was doing to me. I had to talk with it. I had to understand; I wasn't sure what I was doing, but it felt right. So I talked in YouTube or "symbolism" to try to explain my feelings and work through my pain and what is good and right and here to stay for years to come here on earth. I had to be kind to these feelings I had and understand why I was having them even if it was hard to face. It felt like religion to me, and I was releasing the past. I was making peace with all of it. I wanted to be kind to myself.

Three years I'm on top of an ironing board.

Nine years with horse Smokey.

High School Girls choir. I'm at the right second row.

High School choir. I'm in the center second row.

Twenty years with Grand Champion Ram

Twenty-five years.

Thirty-four years.

Thirty-four years.

Elizabeth

Height: 5'5" **Bust:** 34 **Waist:** 26 **Hip:** 35 **Dress:** 4 **Shoe:** 8 1/2 **Hair:** Brown **Eyes:** Brown

Barbizon Model Agency, 7525 Forsyth, Clayton, MO 63105 (314) 863-1141

I'm about forty something in both of these photos.
Elizabeth is my stage name.

To Spill

To spill can cause a mess, so it is better to have a gate or dam for passage to control flow, right? Environmental hazard protected. So past in past, only then an understanding of full picture! Even flow of river over waterfalls to ocean, something very beautiful instead!

Is it possible to live as the Earth for years and then come to life as being? Human process is complicated and requires a lot of balance and tolerance. Earth and human the same process . . .

Theja, the Indian

August 2010

Then something happened . . . I was downloading Native American videos. I was downloading running horses, Mother Theresa. I was calling out to God in the most heart wrenching way ever! My heart had this painful hallow yearning that I could not escape. It was a deep emotion that touched my very soul. How was I going to deal with this? I mean, I pray often, but this time was different. So I went to YouTube. I felt so deprived of hope and faith. God, please listen to me. Have I not been good in your sight? Have you not seen me? I had tears; I sobbed and wept. I thought I was going to die.

I also had these angel cards at home, and I looked at all of them. I talked to those cards and asked, please help me! I thought to myself, I need all these angels, I do. I mean God must be so busy. I would then light a candle and prayed with overwhelming tears of emotion. I mean, I pray often, and most of the time, it is for others, but this time was different. I was in agony, and I was suffering.

Once I was able to calm down, I then went to a Bryan Adams Web site and thanked Bryan Adams for his music. I love his songs, and they have beautiful lyrics, and I like how he sounds when he sings. His voice is so soulful, so tender and passionate. I'm touched deeply by his music, so I thanked him. Bryan Adams writes songs that yearn to express and convey how the soul feels in love, I think. The song I downloaded was

"Please Forgive Me." The video had a young man using sign language while he sang to the song. I thought it was beautiful, and I understood and could imagine his pain.

I know not many people say thank you anymore because it is a lost art to say "please" and "thank you," so I did. Letter writing no longer exists; most comments made now are filled with sarcasm. It has become a competition to see who can be the most sarcastic. I like a little myself, but I also like a kind word or two, and a little of that can go a long ways when you're feeling down. So saying thank you to Bryan Adams was my way of saying thank you to me. Thank you for your hard work; that is wonderful to hear. Sometimes you feel your efforts are never recognized; you are invisible, and your kindness is expected but unrewarded. This was going to have to change for me. So I began to recognize it in myself.

One day, I even had my own burial on Facebook complete with an American flag and a song. I considered myself dead. It was a beautiful funeral. There were Indians there too. Out with the old and in with the new. I even looked at my rights as an American, so I downloaded the American Constitution and Declaration of Independence. I read them all the way through. I was working on myself, so I had to work on feeling good again. I downloaded a video for that too. I started to exercise and ate better. I was addressing all my fears and suffering, and I wanted to heal all of that. I began to feel better. I felt heaven was opening up to me with a smile. I wasn't worried about what others thought about me. I was feeling restored and healthy again.

Then out of heaven came this Indian. Does this part of the story sound familiar? Yes, I said an Indian. He introduced himself as Theja. He wanted to be friends. He said he was from India. He wanted to know about the Indian in the cupboard and the Mother Teresa story. I raised the Indian flag in that one. This spelled opportunity to someone? Are you laughing, or do you have a big question mark in your brain?

I then realized that I should protect myself, so we only talked a little. But for some reason, I was not afraid of him. I wasn't really impressed with him, yet either. I asked him why he was interested in me. He said he liked my pictures, and he liked that I worked with children. I went to his profile, and I could only see his birthday and profile picture and some other photos. He had the same birthday as my ex lover, Gerry. They both had a November birthday on the very same day. I was surprised but suspicious too, so I took it slow. He seemed to enjoy that. Theja is younger than me, and I was sure he had a story to tell as well. He just hasn't told me yet. He said that he wanted to learn about American culture.

We began to talk through e-mail, and I still wanted to be careful. I told him that I didn't want to hurt anyone, and I was a lot older than him. He said he knew that and began to call me "Nancy Ji" out of respect. I looked up "Ji," and the answer I got from Google that day was "sorry" in Hindi. Later, I found out that Theja spoke Telugu, but he also could speak Hindi and Tamil as well as English. Theja didn't know it, but I was relieved to get an apology from him. I needed forgiveness so much. Was this God's way of forgiving?

By some twist of fate, I saw him as my ex lover, Gerry, because they had the same birthday. He called me "Ji" for a long time, and it was as if he was saying sorry every time to me. I know this all sounds strange, but bear with me; this will all make better sense later. You will see. Maybe none of this is suppose to make sense. I was just following my inner voice. I was walking to my own beat, and well, it felt right. You see, I told Gerry sorry, but he never told me sorry, and I just needed that. I did. I know it doesn't make sense.

Theja said that he wanted to learn more about American culture, so I agreed to teach him as long as it was a student-teacher relationship, and he was pleased with that. So I finally made friends with him and let him into my Facebook. We talked every day, and it became fun! He said something nice every day to me. He praised me all the time for my work, with children, and he told me that he liked my downloads. He knew they told a story. We had a very special connection. I was very attracted to him, and I was learning from him as well. When I say that I was attracted to him, what I meant is that we had chemistry. He told me so many wonderful things about India and his culture. It was fascinating to me!

He took my mind off of Gerry, and then I was more able to cope because believe me, I was not coping well. I felt a tremendous pain. It felt like Gerry ripped my heart out or cut me with his dagger. He took it and left me to bleed without even an explanation for why he came and then left. Why did he do that? What did I do? What's wrong with me? What's wrong with him? Why, why, why?

I've been good. I've been too nice to people to have something like this happened to me! But he was not going to let me back into his life, and it hurt like hell! He wanted what I could not give, and I wanted what he could not give. It was not going to work out. He was creating an emotional bond again, and I was not going to allow that to happen anymore. So I had to cut it off!

Well, Theja began to ask me questions about my story that I put together on my Facebook. I wondered why he needed to know. He asked, "What happen to you?" He said, "Spill your story to me." I needed to spill my story to someone, and I believed that he was my guide made into flesh. I wondered to myself, "Did I create him out of my own pain and sorrow for the love that was lost? Do I have this gift?" Theja had to be my guide. He is the Indian I saw as a child. He was kind.

So I bared my soul and told him the story about Gerry. I started with our meeting as young kids in high school. Gerry and I met at a Chinese restaurant. He was a dishwasher, and I bussed tables. I was older than him by a year. He came up to me and introduced himself. He was very confident. He would not leave me alone. He always wanted to talk to me, and sometimes I wondered why he was attracted to me. The pursuit was on.

Gerry later told me that there was a story going around about me that I was raped, and that was why I was so quiet. That story was so untrue! I told him that I was sort of shy but more curious, so I listen to people and learn from watching and using all my senses. I like being with people all the time. I like to learn about them, and I care very much about how they feel. People open up to me and tell me all their stories, and we just met. People often feel comfortable around me, and I'm very easy going and accepting of others.

However, we went out on our first date to a Christmas party that the Chinese restaurant had every year. It all started out wrong. He never came in to meet my parents, and I asked him to do this. It was important for him to first make a good impression on them in order for us to have a good relationship, but that did not happen. My dad was not happy with him, and it was a very bad start if he thought he was going to continue to see me.

Well, we dated for a long time after that party, and I really liked him a lot, and he really liked me a lot. We fell in love, but he wanted to be with me in a physical way. He wanted to make love to me. We had been dating for almost a year now, and we had been working up to that, but I would not give in to him. I told him I had to be married to do that. It was something I was raised on—morals, and I did not want to disappoint my parents. I was afraid of hell, and you know I bought into the whole belief.

Let me first tell you from a women's perspective about sex. It is never just about sex. I know that men have their ideas about what they want, their very structured list about sex and relationships, and of how their relationships should follow a strict code. This code is the rule, and women are expected to follow it, accept that pull away. I know women too can make a man's life miserable with their rules as well.

But please let me tell you how a woman feels about sex. A woman naturally needs that time together to cuddle alone with you, after sex. She wants to know you appreciate her gift to you. With a woman, sex is like letting you into her domain, her Universe. She is trusting you to a secret of herself, and its meaning is profound. So trust is important here. That is why it is so meaningful to first have that dance of desire and seduction because if it is going in the right direction, the two of you will surrender yourselves to each other. It is almost sacrificial and so delicious.

A woman is a creature of emotion and can weep and make love at the same time. If you are there with her at that peak, the two of you will have something that will last a lifetime; it's spiritual. A woman values her body, her soul, her Universe. Her kingdom is where God creates.

So gentlemen, be vigilant of this. I think most women don't just give it away so easily. I think most men want to work for what is so divine to have. Women are aware of this precious choice to make, so do it discerningly. Remember, a woman is having sex with you because it's not just sex. It's a choice to share something deep, something sacred. It could be the next step to making your relationship more exclusive.

Then a man will pull away. He is thinking about all sorts of things. Now, she will have to play that game and not react to this. But it is so hard to do because a woman knows what she gave you, and she will want to explain this but can't. That's why it is important to not give it all away the first time around. You leave him wanting the rest of the story; he wants that bit of you that was kept, and this is when sex becomes so delicious because you did give him a taste but just a morsel of what is to come. And he will delight in finding that if you felt that connection ever so slight. He already loves you, so planning and talking about what you want is so important to have that spiritual experience, small steps and in God's speed.

You know what I'm talking about. Something happens to you after lovemaking. You feel something new, something you either like or don't like. You all of a sudden feel different, and you want to understand it. This can either bring you closer or farther apart. You know something, and you have to explore these new feelings.

Okay, back to the story. So Gerry and I eloped. We went to get a license, and he was younger so his mother would have to sign for him. I was old enough. Gerry's mother did not sign for him, so we went to some friend's house and had them marry us. This was not a real marriage, but it was enough for me. We were married in spirit, and we finally made love, and it was awkward at first, but we were beginners. At first, he was the only one really getting any pleasure out of it. He did pull away at first, but then I got confused and wanted to run. But then he wanted to please me. Well, we wanted to please each other, so we communicated our wants and needs, and it became lovemaking, so it got a lot better.

We decided to keep our union a secret from everyone, especially my parents. We even went out and got rings for that spiritual wedding. Gerry was my first love; I gave him something very special from me. I gave my virginity away to him. We were both virgins to each other, and that is something significant if you think about it, and that is why it is so hard to forget. You are so innocent, and you become so emotionally attached, I suppose.

Gerry was my soul mate, I thought. At the time, I did not realize it, but my father hated him because Gerry did not respect my father, and I told Gerry about this. He tried to be more respectful, but it was too late. My dad did not want me to be with Gerry. He did not like that Gerry did not believe in God. My father did things to try to break us up. He put a time limit on the phone, and I could not stay out with Gerry for very long. There was always a curfew to meet, and believe me; I had to be home on time or no Gerry. That would be the punishment. But even if I would get in trouble, I would do things like sneak out the window to be with him. I was not afraid of getting in trouble. There was no stopping a heart in love, or was it just rebellion?

Gerry was going to go away for college to study to be an engineer. He was so very smart, but my dad could not see him as anything but a kid. I, on the other hand, thought Gerry was everything I ever wanted. We planned to marry and live on his college campus in an apartment. My mom was sure I was marring him to get away from my father.

There was so much disrespect from each of them, and this broke us up. I broke up with Gerry because he was so disrespectful to my father. I wanted to please my father, but I loved Gerry. They could not see what this was doing to me, so I broke up with Gerry and moved out of my parents home so I could go to college myself. What I did was very hard, but I felt it was best. I remember when Gerry said to me, "It's now or never," and I told him, "Never." I guess that holds true today.

A friend of mine called Gerry a vampire. She said he was sucking the life out of me. I didn't know what to think about that. Why was I listening to any of my friends or anyone else? Why didn't I just marry him? Gerry thought I was taking my parents' side. My parents thought I was only thinking about Gerry and not them. Why didn't I marry him? Could it have been his character that turned my stomach?

Yes, there was something else about his character that made me question him. This could have been the one thing that really broke us up. He often talked about having sex with other women. He wanted me to have sex with other men. I couldn't understand this. Why? Wasn't I enough? Was it because we were so young and still needed to know if our love was all that mattered and having someone else would just help us see how wonderful it was? Why mess up a good thing? Sometimes being human really sucks! But this could have been that thing that relationships go through. It's that pull away, that running factor, the go into the cave, the test, and we failed it.

Well, now that I'm older and years have gone by, and I can see that, yes, he was a strong attachment for me, and we had a lot to work out with my parents, but I could hardly break off the relationship with them. They mean so much to me. Dad told me that if I marry Gerry, I could not come home anymore. He was making me choose. Why?

My dad should have stayed out of it, and I have talked to him about this years later, and he has apologized. He knows now how I feel about all this and has asked for my forgiveness. He understands my feelings and feels bad about it all now.

But it was not going to work out at that time. Then here, Gerry was again in my life, and I failed to work it out again because of my morals and our stubbornness and my own ignorance of men. Gerry too was ignorant of women. We just didn't have that understanding between each other. We couldn't communicate our differences. We were all stubborn to a fault. At the time, I just thought that it was the best thing to do. But maybe it was not meant to be, and I just had to recognize that and finally make peace with it. Patience is that of the old and wise, but it does nothing for a young couple in love in the '80s. It's too late to fix, and it's gone forever.

I was a wreck and in pain with a heart that was split in two, so there I was on my computer, downloading my story to God and all his angels to see, hoping for a miracle to save my soul. I was in question about my life and God. I wanted answers to all my questions! I sacrificed love for what? I wanted to jump off a bridge and could have done it easily. And would anyone care? Probably not. Then came Theja. I will get to him in a minute; he just added to my confusion, but he cared. He sensed my hurt. He was a friend, a good friend. But first, I have to tell you about Rodolfo.

Chapter 3

Rodolfo

Theja then asked me if I was married, and I told him the truth. I told him I was separated from Rodolfo for thirteen years. This means that we had separate accounts, and we no longer slept together. We had different bedrooms, and I was on my own with all I did. I had to pay for everything I wanted. I had three jobs and worked hard. Yes, Rodolfo took care of things, but I too took care of stuff around the house. I paid bills. I helped and only made one third of what he made. My father never liked this—about Rodolfo, but it was a modern family. I had to help, and I guess it taught me to be independent. My dad once told me, "Well, you married him; now deal with it." I guess at this point, my dad had learned to let me deal with my own choices in men.

I met Rodolfo after Gerry. I was working at a bank as a teller. He came in on Fridays to cash his check. I watched him, and he was attractive and drove a jeep. I saw him outside the bank as well, and I waved to him, and he took a double take and waved back. That was when he came to my window that following Friday, and my knees started to shake. I knew then he was someone I wanted to get familiar with. He asked me out for a date, and I accepted but then called him and canceled the date. Then I called him back asked if it was okay if we did go out. He asked me if I was asking him out. I said yes, and we started to date.

He was very sweet at first and did impress me with flowers and gifts and made all my coworkers jealous. But he was someone that needed a lot. He was a mess when I met him, but he was kind to me, and I could tell that he needed a friend. We dated a lot, and he took me to some very nice restaurants, and we went traveling together, and he treated me well. I enjoyed all the attention he gave me.

Then we started to ask questions about each other. He told me about how his wife had died in a car accident from a head injury. I saw her picture in his wallet, and I thought it was his wife, so I asked him about her. Well, she didn't die right away. She was in a coma for seven months, then Rodolfo had to sign the papers to take off her life support. She died the same day. I never seen a man cry and feel so much remorse. It was very hard to take. He told me that he never got to tell her good-bye, and that his last conversation with her was an argument about being late.

Rod told me that she, Maria, was his cousin, and his mother did not want them to marry, but they did. His mother did not go to their wedding, but his Uncle, Maria's dad, knew they were in love, and he could not stop them. They never had children together, nor did they adopt.

Then he told me that his wife had a green card, and they were waiting for immigration to call, and while she was in the hospital, hooked up to life support, they called. She could not go with him. Now, he was in a lot of trouble, so I wanted to help him.

After some time, I agreed to marry him at the courthouse in Saint Louis, Missouri, to help him get his green card, again. This was not a real marriage. Oh, and I have to mention this. There was a black man there to marry us. I saw this as a sign. My parents liked Rodolfo because he was respectful toward them. He followed my father's wishes. He had a sense of family. He had an understanding of expectations. I think this is why I liked him. He had a sense of respect. But he did not love me. It was an arranged marriage.

Rodolfo got his dream. He got his green card and brought his family to the U.S. to live; and believe me, I learned a lot. I began to learn

Spanish. I even felt like we were married for real, but he never told me that he loved me. He said that he didn't feel that way about me. He still had pictures of his wife up, and I just had to except that this was the arrangement.

I then one day I saw Gerry again. I then wanted to get back with him, but he didn't because I was with Rodolfo. I tried to tell him why I married Rodolfo, but he didn't understand my behavior. Gerry left again. He was out of my life. I was hurt by this, but somehow, I felt that I deserved it this time.

So then I told Rodolfo I was leaving him. This caused some panic in him, and then he asked me to marry him in a church. I did. I had a church wedding here in the U.S. and then began an adventure to Mexico.

Rodolfo's mother then wanted us to go to Mexico and get married there in a church. So I was off to another country learning another culture. It was an adventure for me. I learned so much, and Rodolfo could see all the humor in it when I couldn't understand.

I remember when we got married. That day while I was getting ready, there was so much going on, and I did not understand Spanish very well yet. I just did whatever I was told to do because it was not my country, and I wanted to learn and live like they do. But there was no rehearsal for the wedding. Rod said, in Mexico, people just tell you beforehand what your part is, and you just do it. He told me that in Mexico, every wedding is the same. So I just did what they wanted. Everyone wanted to help, and I thought that was so sweet how everyone wanted to be involved. There was always someone to offer a blessing or a sweet gift. Yes, it was at times confusing, but it was a large family, and they love you for all your faults and never want you to be unhappy for any reason. If you needed a church, someone helped you with that; if you needed a dress, then someone helped you with that too. Flowers, yes. Someone was always there to give of their heart and wallet. It was beautiful. Why should anyone have to be without a beautiful wedding when there is someone who wants to help you with that? I thought that was so sweet.

There was decorating with tents outside the house in Mexico City. A lady arrives in a bus. In the bus, I noticed that she was driving without a proper bus seat. She had a folding chair for a seat. She was wearing a skirt with heels, makeup, and a smile. There were two other young men there with her—her sons, and they too were in folding chairs sitting down on the bus. There wasn't a proper bus seat anywhere! Well, she was delivering the tent and tables and chairs. After, we helped get that put together with a lot of help from everyone. They left in the bus with folding chairs, and when she made a turn, she held on to the windowpane while she drove a stick shift in a skirt with heels and a smile, and I was amazed.

I had to go to the church with Rod's cousin. He was a police officer in Mexico City. There was a lot of traffic in Mexico, so he just turned on his police lights. He started to yell at anyone in the way. I ducked in the back seat, smiling. I never saw anything like it, but we got to the church quickly.

I remember at the wedding that the organ player was late to arrive. While I was outside waiting to go in, he runs down the aisle with his music, uncovers the keys, opens his book, and starts to play the wedding march. Just in time for the wedding.

At the last minute, the priest did not want us to throw flower petals down in the church. He was this little hunchback priest. He had a bald head and a little hair in a ring around his head close to his ears. He was not very pleasant at all. He complained that he was going to have to clean it up after we left. So Nina, my sister-in-law, told him that she would do it. Thank you, Nina.

However, I walked down the aisle, but I did faint at my own wedding there in Mexico and left an impression on everyone. I'll never forget how I said "I do" to my wedding vows in Spanish and then fainted, and I hit Rod on the way down. I knew I was losing consciousness but could not help myself. When I came to, there was a crowd of Mexicans and a cousin or two with a pamphlet fanning air around me, and Rod's uncle was pinching my neck on my glands by the ears, and I woke up.

I apologized and went on with the wedding and walked down the aisle, white as a ghost. Everyone thought I was pregnant.

It was a funny wedding with a mariachi band, hollering, and tequila—always a lot of tequila and a lot of singing and dancing! There was a tent stretched across the front of the house, and someone came with help to make tacos. The food was wonderfully delicious, but I have to say. I never met so many people that were related. Everyone came, and I met them all! There were children, babies, and people from up the street. It was a block party! The party lasted well into the night, and the next day, everyone was still there to party with leftovers from yesterday. I admired their spirit.

We went on our honeymoon to Acapulco with all his family. His mother was there, his brother, sister, niece, and anyone else that wanted to go. I just went along with it, and Rod said that they just want to enjoy the fun with us. I was beginning to wonder if it was a honeymoon. Rod said that they were going to go to another resort away from us.

But then, on the way there, our car overheated. We had to call for help to take the car to a garage, and that took all day. Acapulco was only five hours away, but we did not arrive till that evening, in a taxi. Let me tell you. We packed that taxi full with bags and people. It was not pretty, but the Mexican way?

When we arrived there, well, the family and friends had to stay too. We just made it work! We shared a hotel room together with his mother and family. Some honeymoon. But now I can look back on it with love and see that I really did marry that whole family. I was in Mexico, and I just learned to smile about it because I knew I was not going to live there, and it was for a short time.

I learned to love the culture and admired their close family bonds. So I had fun and got to laugh at times at the craziness there in Mexico. I really bonded with his mother and all his family there and looked forward to going every time. I even learned Spanish in a very short time. It really was not that hard for me. I fell in love with his family! They were so kind to me, and I wanted to learn all that I could about the

Mexican culture. Having them in my life made it worth being married to Rod. They taught me how to laugh at life and to keep your sense of humor.

I was not sure, but I thought it would all work out just fine. But everyone knows that we are not a couple. Rodolfo never told me that he loved me. He was not affectionate toward me, and I was lonely. I remember lying down in the grass outside our house, looking to the sky, and asking God, "Why can't I have someone to love?" I then looked to the stars and asked for that. I got pregnant with our first child, and I lost it to a miscarriage. I was depressed.

But we have a child together. She became my focus, and she became my reason for living. Thank you, God, for angels, or else I would not have gotten through a very big part of my life. My daughter made me smile again. She helped me see the love in life again. Thank you, God, thank you, thank you.

Then in 1993, I tried to get away from Rodolfo, again. So I called Gerry. We talked, and it was a nicer Gerry, but he had a life with a little girl too. I did not tell him about Rodolfo, but he always knew that our relationship was not a good one. We talked, and then I hung up. I knew he was not available to me.

I was alone, but I had my daughter. And then again, I felt I had to do things for her, so I stayed again to give my daughter a good life. I couldn't go home to my parents, so I stayed with Rodolfo. My responsibility was there—to my marriage, and my daughter. So I put my feelings aside and lived my life for my daughter not knowing that one day, it would all catch up to me.

I remember a few things about our relationship as husband and wife that reminds me of my childhood and things I know that can relate. It was gift giving. Christmas was so much fun. We often had the best time together. We had all his family there every Christmas, and it was so much fun with them there at the house. But I always had a hard time with gifts. Every time I gave Rodolfo a gift, he would take it back to the store. I gave him gifts for a long time, but then it became hard to do because he always took it back. I finally stopped giving him gifts. We often agreed to not gift give. He also gave me gifts, but he was not good at getting it in my size, but I learned to tell him what it was that I liked, and then the gifts became easier to receive. But that was a lesson for me how to ask for what you want.

I received gifts, "intuitive gifts," as a child, but I did not know how to ask for what I wanted. It was as if the Divine would give, but I could not receive. I did not know you could ask for help in understanding or for what you wanted. But you can. You can even ask for help in learning or from the right people to teach you. They just come your way, easily. They look for you and approach you with a smile. You can even be specific in detail about what you want. I had to learn this on my own.

While I was married with Rodolfo, I also had experienced his wife's ghost. She came to me one night while I was in bed. This was before my daughter was born. She came in the bedroom, and I felt her pick my arm off Rodolfo. I woke up and saw something out of the corner of my eye. I was afraid. I really couldn't see a face, but something was definitely there. I woke Rodolfo up and told him what happened. But he laughed and told me that his mother once felt her ghost too. I was not laughing. I wanted to know what to do. I thought I would go crazy if I did not have an answer.

So I enrolled in college, and there was a student there who had an experience that was similar to mine, and the teacher for that sociology class was very open to talk about this. See how God leads you to help when you start to ask for it? I learned a lot from her, and today, we are still friends. She knew this about me—the "intuitive" me, but I still was not able to understand it at all, or maybe I did not want to be different. I was still trying to fit in to what was "normal."

Okay, back to Rodolfo. I think a lot about Rodolfo, and I made a lot of mistakes, but I did well when I picked him as a father for my daughter. He is an awesome father to her, and I feel good about that relationship. I'm jealous too. He tells Lily, my daughter, that he loves her all the time. He has never told me this. He just wasn't in love with me, or he couldn't give to me any love. I was blocked out, and there was a wall around his heart. He was still in love with his wife, and the only people allowed in his heart were his family, but now I understand his love for his dead wife. I truly understand. Nothing can replace his love for her. She was also his first cousin, "family," and "soul mate."

Sometimes your past will catch up to you, and a young lady showed up at our doorstep. I learned about her after Rod and I got married. She is the little girl that he had with his wife's friend after the burial of Maria. You see, Rod didn't always tell me everything. We just did not communicate that well. It was hard to talk to him because he always kept to himself after we got married. I found out about her through the immigration when we went for the interview. They asked me if Rod had any children, and I told them no. Then his lawyer told me that he had a little girl and that he was going to pay child support. I was shocked to hear this. I told Rod that I would love any child that was part of him. I just wish he could have communicated that to me before we got married. I asked him if he wanted to be a part of her life. He said it was best for him to stay out of it. I couldn't understand that. I mean, that is his daughter, his flesh and blood. Why wouldn't he want to be a part of that?

Then she shows up at our house years later, and my daughter meets her. She introduced herself as her sister to my daughter. I didn't get to meet her at all. She was looking for Rod because she wanted to meet her real dad. Rod did finally show up, and he took his daughter out to dinner, so they could get to know each other. When I got home, my daughter was crying. She told me everything that had happen. I tried to tell her what I knew, but she was confused. I wanted Lily to see the bright side to things. Well, now she has a sister she didn't know about, and that is a wonderful treasure to find if she is willing to accept that.

I feel that Rodolfo and I are the couple in the ocean. I'm his wife; that was drowning, but I was not his other half. I feel that I gave him my daughter, which is myself, and he took it. But that marriage taught me how to give, but I gave it all away that I even lost myself in the ocean, and I'll never know how he feels about that because he has never told me. I just drifted away . . .

Now, here I am again with that decision. I'm going to leave; it's the right thing to do. It's the honest thing to do. Theja guided me to see that. He is an angel of God! Theja helped me to remember what it was like to be in love, and I desired that again in my life. I mean, I deserve love, right? I realized that I can do this all by myself. I can! I have to in order to like myself again. I have something to prove to myself, to my daughter to everyone that ever said I couldn't. I'm the "Little Engine that Could" or "Mighty Mouse."

I know I have people in my life that would love to see a woman fail; that seems to be the norm. People like a train wrecked, but I cannot accept that. I also have one or two people who believe I can make a difference. I have to believe that I can do this without failure. That is the truth! I have a story that is different and interesting, and people are going to want to read it. Maybe I can help someone else out there like myself.

Lily

Let me tell you about Lily. She was born on the fourth of July, and she is my firecracker! I remember the night I went in to labor with her. There were fireworks in the sky and inside my belly. I had her naturally and without drugs. It was painful, but I learned how to give birth to her so it would be good for her. I learned Lamaze. I always thought about her first, her needs first.

When Lily came into my life, it was clear that I had a responsibility to her, and I wanted to make sure that I did everything right. Isn't that the way most parents think? You know, you have a lot of important decisions to make about her life, and you want to do it right and for her well-being. No one wants to make mistakes, but I believe that some things are decided before you come to earth. I had no one to really love, so Lily became my focus. I thought she was mine, and I wanted to do whatever I could to do it right. I think I said this too many times, right?

When the doctor gave her to me, I told her, "Welcome to the world. I'm your mommy!" I knew she was the love in my life. I could feel it already. I was thrilled to meet her and to have the opportunity to be her parent. She was beautiful to behold and an "Angel" from heaven. I thanked God that day and every day after for her, and I asked for help many days from God to do well with her. I needed his guidance more than ever, now.

You raise them to how you know, and then you read books, and then you ask for advice, and well, it is an endless cycle learning and mistakes. But I enjoyed raising her! I remember all the warm, wonderful close times we had getting to know each other, as well as the challenging situations in raising a daughter. There are all the times she got sick, and then teaching her when it is night time and she needs to sleep. Oh, and then getting her used to eating what is good for her. I breastfeed her, and she was healthy.

I raised her without having to be too hard on her. She listened to me and was a good child. You know, sometimes you have to take things away and tell her no. I mean how else do they learn? I only disciplined her once with a spanking, but that was because she was not taking her medicine. She was not good at taking it, and she needed to take it to get better, and every time I gave it to her, she would spit it out or let it run out of her mouth even if told her how important it was for her to take it. She would end up in the hospital on an IV just because she would not take it. Reasoning was not working. So here I was with that pink chalky medicine that she hated. She began to pull away and run to hide. I was chasing her. I explained to her that I was worried. I gave her a choice—take the medicine or I would have to spank her, and she would still have to take the medicine, either way.

Let me tell you I even tried the Mary Poppins way. I tried to mix it with other drinks or food, but she always knew I was up to something, and I would lose her trust in me. So I had to be honest with her. So here it goes with the spoon, and I had to gently squeeze her mouth open, and she resisted. I got it in! She spits it in my face! So I sat her down on the couch, and I told her to wait. I needed minute to cool down. Damn, I have to spank her! I didn't spank too hard. I spanked her on the bottom with the back of my hand and gave her a disappointed look, and she then took her medicine. I told her to stay there for ten minutes, and she listened. Lily now takes her medicine with no problem. I never had to do that again. Thanks to God.

Then there was school. School was hard for Lily because I learned that she had ADD. I had to read as much as I could about her condition. But we got her on medicine, she then took off! I'm not the kind of person to turn to drugs, but I had to carefully weigh what was important for her development. It was a very hard decision to make, but I'm glad she got on medicine. It has done wonders for her self-esteem, and she learns, and she is so smart.

Lily and I became inseparable. We were buddies. I loved her! She loved me too, but she didn't want to make friends with anyone. She had one friend, and I felt good about that. But I also wanted her to get out there and make more friends. It's important to develop these relationships. So I began to have parties, and whenever I could, I would put her in classes and invite the neighbors over to play and keep her busy. But she was a mamma's girl. As much as I enjoyed that, I knew she still needed friends too.

Now that she is older, I would worry about her meeting the right man. I pray a lot, and I go to church, and I try to be a good example for her, but I was not doing well in the man department. I worried that she would not know what to do because I haven't been the best example. Rod was not very affectionate toward me. I had one example of love, and I could not talk to her about it. This too sent me out on a quest to prove to her that you must be in good standing and happy with yourself to meet the right one. You must feel that your life does have significance no matter where you are in life and how hard that might be. Have purpose in your endeavors; work hard to achieve your goals. Find the good in all that you've done with humility. I did tell her also to make a long list of requirements and to be complete with all the necessities as well as the fun elements in a man. The longer the list, the better.

I also think it is important to have a list of goals that you want to achieve. Believe in these goals, get involved with the process, and ask a lot of questions. You need to include how you want to be treated by others and how you are going to achieve that. Sometimes you have to earn your peers' respect, but that first comes by having respect for yourself. Have a give-and-take relationship with friends and lovers.

Now that I'm going through a divorce with her father, it has put a dapper on our relationship because I was the one to initiate the divorce. She doesn't understand my position right now. I hope that soon she will see, and I pray I can make her proud of me someday. I have made mistakes, and I do feel very bad about my example. I have to first prove that I am a woman of character and integrity. I want her to see me happy. I have to be honest with myself first, then I will be able to realize or manifest a dream. But I have to accept myself first, and then the dream will come. I owe my daughter that, right? I want her to be proud of me someday.

I can say that I'm proud of Lily. She has showed me her kindness through the years. She is intelligent and intuitive. She is as sensitive as I am, and now she sees her father hurting, so she is there for him. I can understand this from her.

As a mother, I feel I have to give her some advice about the world and love. Go for your dreams and don't let anyone ever tell you no. Those dreams are yours, and only you can fill them. Find a way and the people to help you with that dream. Be thankful for what and who is in your life, and only you can know when you are in love. If you should find true love, I say go for it! Fall head over heels and enjoy that, and don't let anyone change your mind because your heart knows when you are in love. I love you, darling, so very much.

Chapter 4

Theja

Which brings me back to Theja. Okay, this is the part you've been waiting for. Why is he in my life? What happen? How did this collision of souls come to life? I believe we are soul mates. He told me this as well, and at times, I have a hard time believing that I deserve to have him in my life, but I do deserve him. He has made my life wonderful! I'm having a complete connection to the Divine, and it is so pleasing to my soul. I never had so much pleasure. It is at times euphoric. I feel his presence inside my body and inside my soul. He is an orgasmic climax to knowledge that has taken me to the divine spiral intensity of the Universe. He has made me strong in spirit, and I want to share what and how it happened. Do I have your attention? Does all this sound crazy to you? Well, just wait. Are you ready? Because I wasn't. But this really happened!

I told you how we met, but I didn't tell you that I had a picture of myself from when I was only about thirty-four years old. Now, everyone tells me that I look about twenty some years old in that picture. The reason behind that picture was simply to put my best face forward. I needed to do this for me, you see . . . I was beginning to see my own beauty. I was looking at my own true greatness and uniqueness for the world to see.

Well, that was the picture that caught Theja's eye. He told me that that picture spoke to him. He said that my eyes said to him, "Come to me." So then he wanted to meet. I had that pictured up for most of the time that we were getting to know each other. He liked my pictures, but I had to let go of that power of a photograph. I took the photo down and put my real picture up. I took the risk of losing him, but he still stayed attached, and I also was on the internet late at night and up until one or two in the morning. Well, it is about noon over there in India, but I made the comment on a Bryan Adam's site about that time, and Theja saw me there.

November 3, 2010
Balancing the Sun and Moon

Theja invited me to chat with him one day. We chatted shortly before. But I never chatted with anyone else on the computer. He was my first, and I told him this. Like I said, we chatted shortly before this time, but it was brief. We knew at that time we had chemistry. We had this strong connection. I could feel it. He was like a magnet. Something inside me was telling me that he was different. Something told me to just have fun and get to know him. I became so curious about him.

Well, back to the story. You know, I'm in that generation of individuals that are still trying to keep up with their own children, but I'm learning fast! There is a lot I have to learn still, but I'm doing very well. I'm keeping up with my challenges and learning a lot more about computers, and I love it. I even signed myself up in college again to learn more!

He was excited to be with me that day. I took the day off work so I could chat, and he stayed up all night just to be with me. I was nervous, but I tried to relax so I could enjoy being with him. I wanted to have fun, and that was the whole point of the day. He even took me to Yahoo to chat, and he wanted me to send my picture to him—the one he liked the most. So I did. I was so drawn to him.

We mostly talked about India and his culture there. I wanted to know as much as I could about him, and he was pleased to tell me everything. He told me about his childhood and his life now and all that he is interested in—his dreams of doing more. It was all so exciting to me! Our conversations were wonderful and joyful! I felt a psychic connection to him. But we were on the computer for a long time for long hours, and I was losing track of time, but I had to take a break.

I went to the bathroom, and while I was there, I noticed that I had this discharge of vaginal secretions. I was in wonder. I'm in my middle forties, and I have never had anything like this before that I could remember. Well, only when you are having foreplay and ready for sex, right? But there was a lot of discharge, and I had this twitching in my leg, but I was not with anyone, physically. I felt something going on in my body. When I got back on the computer, he asked me "You came?" I was surprised by his question. I knew that maybe we could have a mix up with language, but Theja was doing very well with English, and he was communicating with me just fine. I didn't know how to respond to his question. I liked him and wanted very much to keep him. So I took it slow and went with it and waited for him to take the lead in this very intriguing moment.

Then he said that he was hungry and left to get something to eat. When he got back. He began to talk about things in a way that were so pleasing and arousing to me without mentioning anything about sex. All of a sudden, he was not there. I then wanted to lie down on the couch. The things he said triggered a climax of arousal all over my body. I felt this not only in the general area of the sexual organs but all over my body. I was moving my body to this unusual yoga position, and I wanted to touch my body to please it. I felt out of control. I was breathing deeply. My hips were moving to a rhythm in a circular motion, and heat was moving up my spine and into my head. I was having an orgasm! I could feel it *all over!* I had twitching and spasms! There was large amount of messy vaginal secretions. I thought I was going mad! Is this God? Did I just die? And this must be heaven? Is this magic? I felt confused. In my mind, I was trying to make sense of it all to place some logic to it, but my body was screaming for pleasure. I accepted the gift, and I gave in to these desires. I was off into space, heaven! Oh my god!

I wasn't sure if he felt the same way as I did. I had lost track of time, but I got back on the computer, and he was there waiting for me. He kept saying, "Hello, are you there? Hello?" And he asked me, "Did you feel that?" And I said to him, "Did I feel what?"

Now, remember, I was a bit afraid of what was going on. I could not admit to this. Theja was disappointed in me. I could not assume that he had the same experience. I was in disbelief about the whole thing. He was so disappointed in me. He was angry at me, I think. He wouldn't even chat with me anymore for a while. I was feeling sort of out of control, like someone was telling me to pay attention, that this was a rare occurrence. But we did chat again, and I realized then what was happening. We chatted more times after that, and I was sure that we were having an awesome bond to something beautiful—*big*. It wasn't until months down the road that I was able to talk to him honestly about this. I really feel this physically, and he does too. I really have this physical or chemical reaction in my body. It is hard to explain. It's this energy between us that makes us want to be with each other all the time. It's joyful. We are always relieved to see each other when we video chat now, and I don't want anyone else even with our so-called circumstances.

Theja has moved in to my Facebook. What I mean is that we have e-mailed each other for over a year every day, twice a day. Like I said, we video chat often, and the feeling is wonderful! There is a connection here, and he often tells me that we are soul mates. We are holding on to each other and still working through this relationship. We cannot help how we feel. It's hard to think about anyone else because we feel so connected.

I talked to a professional friend about this and she said that we needed a union, a physical manifestation or bond of balanced harmonics of yin and yang—the male and female balance of both sexes. This is a very serious partnership made with God, and we become earth angles at that point and serve a purpose on earth for the greater good and are guided with that purpose to help others. I believe I'm ready for that, but we need to decide what our purpose is and what roles we will play as male and female because there has to be a male and female energy together. We are balancing the sun and the moon. This is what all the pyramids have been built on this experience. You balance your life where it needs to be balanced. I had even more questions that needed answered. I became a Google and a YouTube junky.

We are soul mates, and we have a connection to the Divine. I didn't realize just what was happening to me, to us! It is so strong. It is so intense; I don't know how else to explain it. Soon, we both got sick together. We had flu like symptoms. Theja was sick first, and then I got sick. I became so curious. I needed to know what was going on, and this was the beginning of my journey to find the answers to "what is happening to me.?" It became a madding experience, and I often wondered why this is happening to me. I can have Theja or this Divine experience anytime, and I don't have to compromise anything. It's here for me and Theja whenever we need each other. Maybe it was our time and our fate to meet and learn this. But I'm learning to ask for what I want now. I felt sorry for not telling Theja the truth that day, and I apologized to him, but he knows now and understands me. I know that he went out on a limb to ask me that question, but we have a bond now. Theja even told me about a movie that was made in India, *Saagara Sangamam*. It shows the very same bond between souls like ourselves and that very same divine experience. It's the only movie I ever saw that captures it in a small scene or two. I mean I understood it. I knew what was going on between those two.

I then began to research as much as possible about this. I read and Googled more than I ever have in my life. I found out that I was having a *kundalini* awakening. This is a profound spiritual realization or enlightenment experience. I also researched some more and found out about psychic mediumships. This is where another soul enters your body to fill its desires, and Theja is a man twenty years younger, so I feel his urges and his maleness. I know him without being with him. I feel him.

I became so aware of my life and the people in it. I became so driven to fix things that needed to be fixed for the better of the people around me and myself. I became focused on improving my life, and I saw a clear path in order to do it. I saw beauty in everything around me, and I understood the golden ratio and what it meant to me. At times, I wondered what is wrong with me and why I am so driven to do what I'm doing, but I cannot help myself. I feel as if I am being guided to do the things I'm doing. This must sound crazy to you, but there is no other way to explain it. I was being guided, and Theja was the one that evoked this in me. It was like I wanted to remember something. So if you think that is crazy, wait till you hear this . . .

I went to India to visit Theja. He invited me, and off I went to be with him. I had to meet him. I had this uncontrollable desire to be with him. He told me that he felt the same way. We thought about each other day and night. Theja could read my feelings well. He always knew when I was sad or happy or confused. It wasn't an obsession. It was a real kinship of souls. He told me that in order for him to feel happy, I must be happy. I began to try to be more optimistic and work through each emotional trauma and release it as soon as possible so Theja wouldn't feel sad too or confused. We also understood the fact that we were different but the same. We could not help how we felt about each other.

I first have to tell you that it wasn't a hard choice for me to make to go to India. I mean here where I live, everyone you talk to is miserable. I wanted to share my story with my friends and relatives, but they are all so miserable. I couldn't begin to tell them what I was going through. Many of my friends are talking about how hard it is for them—moneywise, their health, relationships—and then when you turn on the TV, it's there in your face again—people suffering, no cheer, or happiness. Who do you help first? It seems the only thing I could do was listen to their stories. Well, it's enough to make you want to leave the country! I just needed to get away from all that and start with Nancy first. So I jumped.

Theja and I made plans for the trip through Facebook, like when I should go and what hotels to stay at, what I should wear, And where we would go once I got there. This is a whole new country to me. I needed his direction, and he told me just what to do. I listened to him because I wanted the trip to be successful. We planned it together, and it was nice to have someone that cared about my input. I asked a lot of questions and read about the places that we were going to see. I even read about some of the gods and the lengthy stories. I was very interested in Lord Shiva and the cosmic dance, but I also liked the Hindu gods—Venkateswara, Ganesha, Hanuman, and Buddha. They are only a few favorites, and there are so many—three hundred thirty million gods and goddesses in the Hindu culture. Well obviously, god is everywhere in India. There is so much to learn, and their stories are very captivating and lengthy.

It was an awe-inspiring trip. I left on March 19, 2011. There was a strong "super moon" that evening. Maybe that had something to do with it. But even today, I feel his pull, but I wanted to just see him for real. We were both excited and could hardly wait to meet. I was worried that he would not be pleased with my appearance because I am so much older than him. I worried about that a lot. He said he was worried I would be disappointed with him and his age. I told Theja that none of this made any sense, and it was not logical to travel to India. It had no reasoning. I mean we never talked to each other on the phone or video chat until the day I left for India. He knew this as well, but he told me not to think about it. But we were both in for an experience.

For the trip, I had bought Indian pajami dresses so I would blend in with everyone there. I wanted to honor Indian traditions, so when Theja said it was a good idea to dress like everyone else, I did it out of respect. Well, it was obvious that I was American, but everyone there was so nice and so hospitable. I felt very welcomed. Everyone there wanted to make a good impression on me, and I never felt so good about a meeting before. I know this took guts to do, but I was driven to learn, and everything went well for the trip. I told Theja again that none of this was logical or made any sense, but there I was in India, with a man that truly wanted to meet me as well.

It was a long flight, twenty-two hours in all, and I was smart about it. I talked and made friends along the way. I made sure I never walked alone. I was always with someone. There were a lot of professional people to talk to, and I slept a lot too.

I called Theja, and that was the first time I ever heard his voice. He sounded nice. I could tell he was a good person, and I liked him. I called him once before I left Saint Louis and then in New York, and we talked about our first meeting. He wasn't sure how to greet me. Were we to shake hands or hug? Theja said that no one hugs in India, or it would be awkward. But I wanted to hug him. Okay, our first culture shock.

Then I finally arrived in Hyderabad. My phone was not working. I looked for Theja, but I must have missed him. I then got a taxi to my hotel with another kind gentleman that I met, and he was with me and gave me company to the hotel. I thanked the gentlemen, and I paid for our taxi. I was reminded of the reality of our world and had to go through a security check before I could go in to the hotel. There were a lot of those security checks in India. They even checked the taxi underneath with a mirror.

I was tried and needed a shower, so I showered. Then I called home from the hotel phone to let my daughter know that I was fine and arrived safely to India. Then Theja called. He knew which hotel I was staying in. Then he and a friend arrived to greet me.

Theja was shy. Can you believe it? Here is this six foot, tall gentlemen, and he was shy? Theja walked in; our eyes met. I only saw his eyes. I smiled, and I invited them in to sit. I asked them if they wanted a drink of water. It was a bit awkward, so I played hostess. I had to step it up and make everyone more relaxed. I asked if they were comfortable. The tension was strong, but they seemed relaxed. Theja introduced his friend to me. We talked a little about my trip on the plane, and then they asked me what had happened. I explained everything, and then we talked for some time about what we were going to do the next day. It was late, and I started to nod off to sleep on the bed. I could tell that they wanted to stay, but I didn't feel right about it yet. Theja's friend said that they would go and meet me at the hotel after I rested. I got up and helped them to the door, but I couldn't help myself. I had to give Theja a hug and a smile. He was surprised by my actions and moved quickly away from me. This was a culture shock for Theja and me. I couldn't understand why he moved away. What's wrong with a hug? Where I live, people hug each other if they are comfortable with that. I mean children hug you once they get to know you, and you hug your friends. I could see that; I had a lot to learn about Indians, and Theja had a lot to learn about Americans. How was this going to work out?

We went to sightsee that next day in Hyderabad, India, to see the Fort. We first went to out for breakfast, and we talked about everything. I wanted to know as much as I could about India in the short time I was there. So I asked questions, and I did read a little before I went so I would be able to know more. But the best way to learn is by doing, am I right? Theja liked my attitude. He then told me that he and his friend had to sleep in the car last night. I felt bad about that and told Theja to please not to do that again. He and his friend were welcome to stay in the hotel with me. I could see that they were very interested in me as well, not so much in a romantic way but just a fascination. I was feeling more comfortable with them any way.

Then it was off to the Fort. Theja's friend did have a car to get around in. Traffic was heavy, and there were people everywhere. I once saw someone walking in this traffic, and it was amazing to me how no one hit this person. There was the sound of horns everywhere—motorbikes—and the yellow taxi with three wheels.

We first ate breakfast that morning in a small restaurant before the Fort. We ate rice with potatoes in a hot yellow sauce with bread and then curd or yogurt.

Then we went to the Fort and walked around a lot. I learned about some of India's history. So after that, we went back to the hotel for a short nap. Theja slept in a chair, and his friend slept on the bed away from me. It was a king-size bed, so there was a lot of room. Then I peeked at Theja and saw that he was looking at me too.

Then we got up, and they took me to see the Buddha statue and a park that evening before dinner. It was a clean park, and we walked around looking at people, and there were vendors and snacks being sold and a lady selling flowers for your hair. Theja bought me some. They were jasmine and smelled so sweet. Then we walked some more to the boat to see the Buddha, and Theja's friend was walking ahead of us. It was getting dark, and Theja gently held my hand for a moment. It was so sweet. I just decided to live the moments without judgment, and I was glad I did.

Then after that, we ate delicious Indian food at this very nice restaurant. The waiter took our order on a cell phone, and the kitchen got our order as soon as we said what we wanted. I thought this was very high tech. I've been to New York and other cities but never saw this before. I ordered chicken biryani. It was very spicy but so good, and the flat bread that was served with it was fresh and wonderful. It melted in your mouth. Theja taught me how to eat Indian style. You eat with only your right hand. He showed me how to use your fingers to push your food into your mouth. I was grateful for his guidance. There were forks and spoons, but we ate Indian style. You then washed your hands at a public sink there at the restaurant.

Theja stayed the night in the hotel because he said that he did not want me to be alone. I took my sandals off and then got comfortable in front of the TV on the bed. Then Theja came and sat on the bed next to me. He moved in close, and we held each other. I was surprised. He was wanting to cuddle; I wanted to cuddle as well, but we kept our clothes on and slept all night and the next day together. It felt good, but I wanted him, and I could tell that he wanted me too. It was so intense. The next morning, his friends were at the door, but we did not answer. We just cuddled and forgot to eat. We forgot about time, and it was like we were melting together.

Then we had plans go to Tirupathi, so we got up and got ready. We took turns showering and had a pleasant time helping each other get ready to leave. I went with Theja to the train station, and we rode on one of those little taxi with three wheels. We sat close together, and every once in a while, he would glance at me. We rode a train to see the famous temple, just Theja and I. I really liked the train ride. Theja told me stories about Indian religion. I was sort of listening but also so curious about everything else going on around me. I watched him as he watched me. He told me that I look about twenty some years old. I told him thank-you.

We met these really sweet ladies. We made our acquaintances, but they were curious about me. They liked my Indian dress. They were surprised at how old I was. I thought that Theja just made me look younger. They wanted to share their food with me. I was so honored by their gift and thanked them for sharing. I put my hands together to show respect to them. We talked about a lot of things, and one of them even introduced her son to me before we got off the train.

Theja and I had a good time on that train. He also told me stories about the Indian gods, but I was not listening. I was too caught up in all that was going on around me. He knew this, and often he could tune right into me, and he just knew I was wondering off. I was surprised by his ability. He could read my every intention, and we even imagined in our minds what it would be like together. We talked about being a couple. Then I got up to take a break, and Theja followed me. As I was finishing up washing my hands, Theja was waiting for me, and there was this very intense moment. He took my hands and looked into my eyes. I felt a vibration stir deep within my soul. It was that presence of God again. Oh my lord!

We slept in different beds across from each other and often stared at each other and smiled when our eyes met. I held my arms out as if to give him a hug that evening. It is a pleasant, fulfilling relationship. I truly felt at peace. The rocking of the train on the tracks put us both to sleep.

I will explain what the beds look like. When you get on the train, there are benches. There are three beds in all stacked on top of each other on the wall, and they are cushioned. The one closest to the bottom is the one that everyone sat on till time for bed. Then everyone works together to make the beds. Two of them have to be fold down on steel rods that hold the weight. Like I said, they stack. Once that is done, someone then comes around with clean white sheets in brown paper to put down on the beds. Everyone cooperates and fixes their own beds by taking turns or helping each other. This is how they travel in India on a train, and this was middle class, and they did have air condition. I had a very pleasant experience.

When we got to Tirupathi, we went to see the Lord Venkateswara to pray, and I to say thank you as well. The smell in the air was something of incense and flowers. It was enchanting and mystical to me. There were a lot of beautiful flowering trees and bushes. The homes there were impressive, and the streets were well kept. Many of the women were wearing saris with their long braids and beautiful gold jewelry on their golden skin. They had toe rings and earrings that looked like bells, ankle bracelets, and of course, bangles. I paid close attention to all of it and just took it all in. I want to learn Telugu, but there really was no need because everyone there can speak English. I guess that is because they use English in business, and India just got their independence in 1947. I was relieved but knew I still wanted to learn Telugu. Theja was teaching me.

Tirupathi is a Hindu temple, and it was crowded. But we waited in line, and it took us about two hours to see Lord Venkateswara. Theja and I always had plenty to talk about while waiting, and he always had his eyes on me. Yes, it was crowded, but people used their manners. I got a smile from people when I smiled at them. Theja and I often glanced at each other, and his eyes would penetrate my soul.

We finally got to see Lord Venkateswara. The ladies there guided me to him, leaving Theja behind. I was surprised but then giggled a little under my breath to see Theja there being held back. He kept watching me, and I kept my eyes on him as well, and he smiled at me, and then I felt better. Then my attention was on what the ladies were saying to me. They then pointed to this small entry where you could see this black statue for only a brief moment. I bowed and quickly asked for what I wanted and said thank-you to Lord Venkateswara. Then I found Theja. We gave money to the temple on the way out. Theja and I then ate rice and yogurt there too. I was afraid, but I also wanted to have the whole temple experience to really be involved, and Theja helped me with that. I was grateful to him.

Theja and I did sleep together in the hotel in Tirupathi. When we first got to the hotel, I noticed that there were two smaller beds. But Theja moved the beds together right away. He was, however, a gentleman, and we did not have intercourse. That again is something that I need to explain. Sorry to disappoint you, but there was no physical penetration. I was still confused about a lot and wanted to do the right thing, and I was still married, and then I did not understand his culture yet. I did not want to cause any wrong vibrations into his or my universe. I had to think about karma, his way of life. But I did want him. So we just held each other, and we slept the whole night and almost a day in bed. It was like nourishment for our souls. The attraction was strong and mutual, almost unbearable. We had this tantra or tantric experience which is this orgasmic energy. It's in the mind, body, and soul. That's the energy we feel. It's all over. We could feel the flow of energy from the universe. Theja calls it paradise or heaven. It felt good to be next to him, and we hardly talked. When our eyes met, it was a soul connection that radiated over many life times. I wanted to remember what our past connections were. We had this communication of minds. Telepathy was going on for sure, and we have that still. I'm still in amazement about the whole thing.

I was only there for six days and had to leave. It was hard to go and leave him. I remember walking and turning around to look at him, and I waved one last time before I left at the airport. His eyes were so piercing. I felt that energy, that strong vibration again . . . I realized that I really loved him. Could I be falling in love with him? Is this another crazy idea? I'm beginning to see a pattern here. Well, why couldn't I? I began to fantasize the idea of having him for a lover, but I was so confused. I asked God, "How is this fair? Why would God do this?"

Theja and I e-mail every day. I wake up to his text message. It's like getting a kiss while I slept. I now call him once a week to talk. We video chat, and I'm sure we are part of the divine universe experience. I've read about this on many sites and found it hard to believe that I'm in a relationship like this.

But I am, and I plan to enjoy it and learn as much as I can about all this. I mean, God gave this to me. I want it. I accept the gift. Believe me; this is all new for me. I think I'm feeling the male side of myself, but I'm still a woman with the nurturing side very much intact.

Theja suggested that I read about Buddhism, and I did, and it talks of an enlightenment, and I'm sure this is what I'm going through—some kind of self-realization. I had to learn that I had all I needed right inside myself. I'm the miracle! I've also read about tantra. This is somehow connected to that "energy" we feel with the divine god source, and I believe that I have found that to be what had happened to me and Theja. We had to meet to have this experience. We are soul mates. We are learning about the Divine and how that is found within ourselves, our purpose. We are in a God relationship, and it's so beautiful. I never had anything like it, and it feels so wonderful, so marvelous!

Well, with that said, yes. With Gerry, it was good, but something about his character was not right. Theja and I are sharing a real soul mate relationship. But that intense need I had for Gerry actually made him repulsive of me. So I had to pull myself together and look within to find my strength of my own desire. This is important to know because I think I had to have that experience first to have the one I am having with Theja. The crushing experience was the enigma—the part of the riddle to finding a soul mate. So I had to feel first good about myself, look within, and know that I was worthy of love and heal. It was my real soul-searching lesson.

I'm the hero! I just had to first clean up my life and lead myself to the goal—happiness—even if my life was not reflecting that. Gerry could sense my neediness, and that caused him to leave me. Gerry did not want me, and that was a very painful, and then I started to send out messages to the world of my experience. I cried out to God about my pain, and then I got Theja. The same vibration as mine; he is not letting go, and I believe him. Theja, likes the connection we have and is not running away from me. We share the same soul substance.

But I had to first pick myself up, dust myself off, and feel better about myself, which means I needed to see the positive side of myself. I started to look at life in so many ways. I understood the function of domain and range. This was the negative turned into the positive. I understood what the golden ratio was and it's beauty in nature. I saw it all around me and worked that into my life as well. It was the Buddha path I was walking, and along the way, I found serendipity. I needed a mirror to look at myself. So that was when I got Theja, my other half, and I liked what I saw. But I had to look at the negative too, but that wasn't so bad.

Theja says he has a hard time showing love. I think he does just fine—showing his love or maybe I just understand him. I can hear his thoughts, and I read his emotions, so there is no need to express those thoughts of love. I feel them from him, and it feels like heaven to me.

I understand our connection, and it is an awesome one. And I know that Theja feels it too. But by the time I met Theja, I had to rationalize this feeling and knew that he was there to teach me to find my own understanding, my own sole purpose. I am my own hero. However, Theja is strong in himself and believes that we need to stick together to achieve our dreams and find our purpose. We support each other. We praise one another, and that is what I read in all the soul mate sites. You need to find your purpose. I now know what mine is, and it is to help others, like myself and Theja.

Theja says our purpose is to show the world our love for each other and stick together through everything till our last breath, so we can meet each other again in the next life. The next life together will be absolute. This is what we are working on, and we help each other with life's challenges. Theja was there when I needed him most. I love him for that.

Working on this book has helped a lot, and I believe that I was meant to write about this experience for others in the same situation to help them deal with their separation till they can meet together as one. We are soul mates, and that is the real significance of it all. We want to be with each other. If it is God's plan, then we will have to see how it works out. As you can see, I'm still struggling with this. At times, the separation can be very painful because I miss him. The truth is you cannot help how you feel about someone or who you fall in love with. Now that I've found him, I want to be with him and no one else. Theja says that he feels the same way.

But I know that meeting Theja was my destiny, and we were supposed to meet. I had to work out a past life that needed to be settled in order to move on to a happier place—emotional, mentally, spiritually, and definitely physically. Theja is my soul mate. We are trying to work this out. Believe me; it has not been easy to do. At times, it's maddening. I mean, he lives in India, and I'm in the U.S. He is a man who is younger than me, but that in itself is not a bad thing. And the attraction is strong. He's all the man I will ever need.

We cannot help how we feel about each other! We compared ourselves to everything, that this relationship could be but for now. We see each other as soul mates, with much to be worked out yet—step by step—with many more life's challenges ahead. I will be there for him. I love him so much.

As frightening as that is to me, I still cannot help myself. So I will honor it instead. As big of a risk as that might be, I still cannot help myself from loving him the way I do. It is like loving myself. But he is the perfect man for me. He has that something that only a soul mate could understand. It was so incredible how we met and then got together. It's so amazing and awesome to know that you really meet your soul mate across many oceans and continents through the internet. That absolute feeling that he is the one. No one else compares; no one else can compare.

This is Theja, my soul mate.

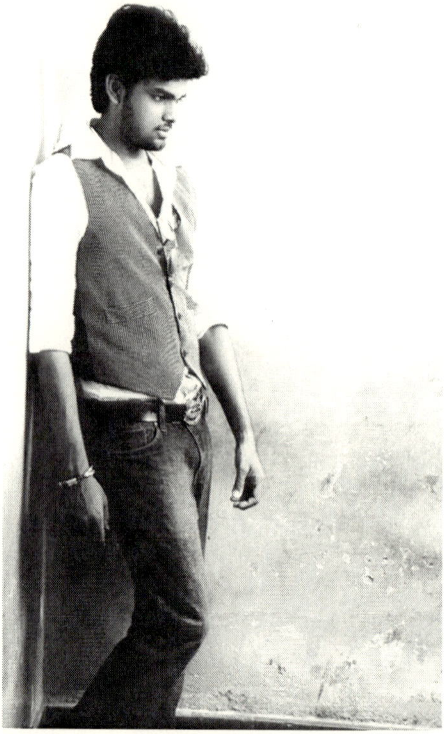

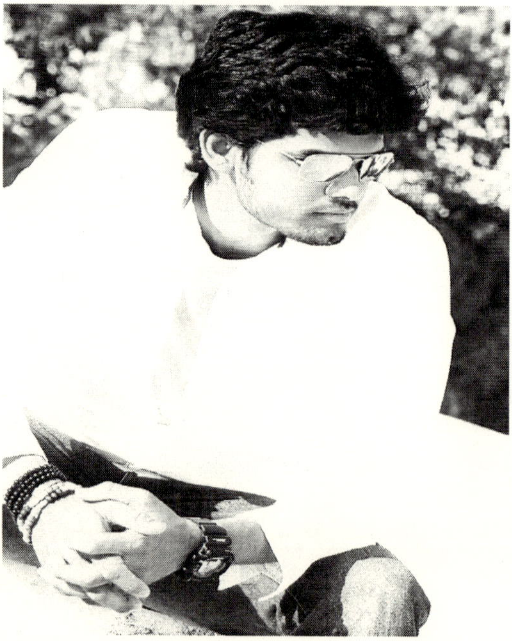

Chapter 5

Myself

I am now in the process of a divorce. There is a lot of negative around that. I know that I am only one person, and there is a lot stacked up against me because I don't have a lot of education. My parents thought I would marry, have children, and then be happy. That was the normal thing to do in my generation. I will get back in school again after the dust settles.

But I have to be optimistic! I believe that I have an amazing story that needs to be shared with the world. Yes, this crazy story! But because of my headstrong generation, I am able to stand and shout out that you need to be an individual even if it is taking a risk on an idea. Believe in your own aspirations. Be who you are. You have a purpose, and mine are that of the intuitive sort. I am an empathic or Indigo of sort. I "feel" most of the time everything around me! I just don't see, hear, touch, smell, taste; but most of it, I "feel" and "know."

I hope my story can help those people like myself. The purpose of writing down my childhood and everything was to give you a good look at how normal I can be and how much the same I am. But I have an understanding of nature and beauty in all realms, but at the same time, I'm a bit odd, but I'm okay with that. I'm just very curious. This could be my own humble form of esoteric training.

This book was put together to help find my way out of a maze. Yes, it is a transition period. I don't know much about transits other than my astrologer said I was in one. That is when you deal with your karma, your spirit guides, and your life changes. That is a huge learning. You get what is yours, even your soul mate. It's like playing a country record backward. You get everything you lost back. You just need to know how to look, and you will need help with that. An astrologer is very helpful, but you are in control of your life—free will. You understand your own life and its challenges you have to face. You have to do the work. You become more spiritual; you are drawn to God because you are suffering. You have to use your intuition, and sometimes that is hard when the beast inside you wants to control everything. And that beast must be trained.

Sometimes you have something called "retrograde motion," and I'm pretty sure I was having this. Ever heard of déjà vu? It's when a transiting planet moves over a particular spot in a natal chart and then turns retrograde and passes over the same spot again before it then goes "direct" again and passes over the spot for a third time. This brings a prolonged period of change into your life. You recognize the pattern, and you see and learn the lesson.

There are a lot of confusion and misunderstandings, but you have to do the work and take risks. Kind of like watching the movie *Groundhog Day*. You have the desire to change. Improve your life where it is needed. You find your purpose, you deal with yourself, and sometimes you don't always like what you see about yourself. It's hard to look at yourself and admit your weaknesses. I mean you really see the worst of yourself. Believe me, it's not pretty to look at your worst insecurities and your bad habits. You have to bare your soul sometimes to a trusted friend or soul mate. That's when you turn the negative into a positive. You go back to those old relationships and habits again and look at how you can handle them in a positive manner. You try to find where it is that you belong in these relationships. But in retrograde, you seem to be more aware of what you are learning, so you have a little more control. You don't let "anyone" take advantage of you in any way. It's a great learning period, and you will be surprised how easily you recognize everything and still get confused, but you now "know" what to do because you "feel" what is right.

My worst one is the disrespect I put up with from my coworkers, friends, students, parents, ex, daughter, and even my soul mate. I had to address them all. Make sure things are fair and handled, so I don't feel left out, forgotten, mistreated, and turn them into, acceptance, concern, forgiveness, community, and compassion. You have to get in there and get involved with the process. Don't just sit there and witness a wrong doing against you or anyone else. You wiggle around, looking for the right answer. So have strength and roll up your sleeves and work for a better change. Be happy and find cheer and good in all that you do. Be optimistic, take a deep breath, and smile and relax. It's going to be okay; you can get through it.

Well, you know that Theja is the Indian guide that came to me as a child when my grandfather died. The Indian was a clue that God put in there to find my guide. Theja is my gift, my soul mate, that God sent, but I was unable to accept it at that time. So he came back as the man he is today, but he has always been there; he never left. I sometimes think that Theja was my grandfather. Grandpa had a strong spiritual connection with me. Before my grandpa died, he gave me a Bible, and I still have it today.

It took some time, but I have opened my arms to Theja with great joy, and I now accept any and all gifts that I have. Because I understand it so much better now, he is my connection to God. Theja gave me a hand when I was drifting in the ocean alone. He understood my longings, my yearnings to understand the cosmos, the whys, and what fors, and the enigma. Theja taught me that you are not alone, and there is someone out there for you, just for you. It's God's humility.

I often wonder to myself how can I show my love to Theja physically. Now that I have this love and he's oceans and continents away and unavailable in the physical, what do I do? How do I handle this? But there are many creative ways, poems, songs, music, buildings, bridges, paintings, movies, and books. The list can go on and on when you think about it. Many people have done this for a loved one, a soul mate. Out of the emotion for the absolute, divine love comes creation! That's why I wrote this book; it is our baby. It has to be my greatest work—my masterpiece, and I will be writing another one soon.

So if you're not sleeping at night and listen to that small voice in your head, you can find your soul mate. Maybe he is on the other side of the world. You can live your dream as well; you only have to listen and follow your heart. If you think about it, then you will be distracted by other things in the universe and get confused. Sometimes divine love makes no sense. It's like the blind teaching the blind which makes total sense to the heart. Helen Keller once said, "The most beautiful things in the world cannot be seen or heard but felt with the heart."

The horses, well, what do they mean? They are the chaos that had happened related to my mother's accident. These horses had no one on them, so it was chaos. I wanted to turn this into a positive, so I looked up Plato for some advice. I found something awesome. Plato wrote about the three pleasures, and it goes something like this.

"First is sensual or physical pleasure of which sex is a great example. A second level is sensuous or esthetic pleasure, such as admiring someone's beauty or enjoying one's relationship in marriage. But the highest level is ideal pleasure, the pleasure of the mind. Here, the example would be Platonic love—intellectual love for another person unsullied by physical involvement."

"Paralleling these three levels of pleasure are three souls. We have one soul called appetite which is mortal and comes from the gut. The second soul is called spirit or courage. It is also mortal and lives in the heart. The third soul is reason. It is immortal and resides in the brain. The three are strung together by the cerebrospinal canal."

Now, here are the analogies using horses. Are you ready? Okay, here it goes . . . "Appetite, he says, is like a wild horse, very powerful but likes to go its own way. Spirit is like a thoroughbred, refined, well-trained, or power-directed.

And reason is the charioteer and goal-directed, steering both horses according to his will."

Now each one of these horses plays an important role, either separate or all together, one at a time or two at another time, but the wise thing to know is when to use each one and how at the right time. So sometimes reason cannot lead, and then it is time for courage, and you must follow your heart. But it was the appetite that started everything.

The scar on my mother's body from the horse accident is the meeting with Gerry. I was "crushed" by the meeting, the repulsiveness of us once again. He is something of a twin flame, I thought. But he was the illusion of love. In real life, he is a twin; he has an identical twin brother. That sent me to meet Theja, my guide who I know is my true match in soul—my soul mate. We are of the same soul substance.

My mother telling the story after the chaos is this story to explain to my own daughter the chaos of this divorce and my soul's journey with my guide to God. Which would be my mother getting back on top of the horse that nearly killed her. Which is finally being able to have control with mind, body, and soul.

I have always been blessed in the "physical realm," and that is why it came through in this way. I understand creation in a God's sense. This is how miracles are made through emotions, tears, dance, and any movement in the physical along with deep heart wrenching emotion. There has to be that element.

Later after my grandma died, we found her journals, and I read them and found out that on the day my mother had her accident, an old boyfriend of hers had died in a plane accident on the same day at the same time. There was an illusion between the two of them. I don't think they ever had a physical bond, but it was an illusion. But my dad was there for my mother, and he loved her and held on to her. He prayed to God in the most heartfelt way to not lose her. I know this was a transition period, but my mother is a living miracle. Thank you, God.

My grandma guided me there to look at those pages, and it was important information to know. She too helped me see what was real and honest. I believe that most of my childhood was to learn integrity of character. I had all the right people.

I know that I was to meet Rod and Lily. They have taught me about having a sense of humor in life and about giving and receiving and how to ask for what you want. This somehow was hard for me to learn. I never felt worthy of God's gifts. I had to learn that. I still want to have a healthy relationship with my daughter, and I hope God and his angels can help me with that. I want her forgiveness. I'm thankful for Rod. He had been a mountain to climb. Why did I have to climb that mountain? I think it was to learn how to respect myself and to learn how to be independent to find my value.

I received gifts, "intuitive gifts" as a child, but I did not know how to ask for what I wanted. It was as if the Divine, would give, but I had no idea how to receive and/or get what I wanted. I did not know you could ask for help in understanding or for what you wanted or had received. But you can. You can even ask for help in learning or from the right people to teach you. They just come your way, easily. They look for you and approach you with a smile. You can even be specific in detail about what you want. But God sends them and not always how you want, but it happens. I had to learn this on my own.

I believe this connection I made with Theja was supposed to happen. We had to, and it was not some accident but yes, fate. We have been trying to figure this out and why there is such an unbelievable magnetic connection. We have discussed everything from mother: son to father, daughter, friends, soul mates, and couples. But maybe we are all of the above; the connection we have is deep. We have lived many lifetimes in many scenarios, and that is why we are having such a hard time sorting and analyzing the relationship because it is a divine soul relationship. It is this, and it feels so honest and real and familiar. It is a relationship that is based or grounded on unconditional Love. I feel him in my body, my heart, my head, and my soul. I look at him, and in his eyes, I see his soul. I recognize him; it's familiar to me. I know he loves me.

Theja believes that he is the miscarried child I had before my daughter, Lily. This could be true, but I cannot help how I feel about him! The funny thing is that we both understand that we are not really connected in that way on the physical plane. It is spiritual. It's all together different—our relationship. God put us on different continents and in different cultures. I think about it, and it is a miracle that we met and how we found each other. But God did this not to separate us; he wants us to try to get to each other. I know it's hard, and our circumstances seem adverse but not impossible because love makes it possible.

Before I met Theja that summer, I bought these bangle bracelets. I don't know why I became interested in them, but I was drawn to them. I wore them and got compliments when I did. I started to take notice of things like that. I also became interested in yoga. It was like the universe was trying to get my attention toward India. The universe was communicating with me, and Theja helped me learn how to communicate with the spiritual realm and to understand what is enlightenment. We know what we are feeling, thinking, and reading. We do it without knowing sometimes. It's amazing!

However, he is in India and a man with a cell phone connected to Facebook, from a family there, and with big dreams and plans for his future. I am a woman living in the U.S. looking for her soul and found it or he found me. He can make me feel so wonderful, and he has the same reaction about me. He says he is coming here to study to get his master's degree because it's a dream of his. We will have to sort through the relationship, but he again will be in another state. I invited him to come and visit me any time. I know he will always be in my life. I feel that he will be there when I die; I really do because that's just how real it feels! Theja helped me when I was alone in the ocean adrift. He helped me get back on the horse, and now this book is our baby.

This lesson I learned has the understanding of world peace in it, and I truly believe it does. We are all on the same planet and feel very much the same and only need to remember our manners and have respect when dealing with each other's culture. We all have pain and loneliness. We all share joy, and we all want freedom and all the human characteristics written in the law of being human! This need must be met in us all men, women, children, animals, and environment. It's all connected to this place we call home, "Earth".

I feel that the five-dollar bill that was given to my father after the accident stands for freedom for all humans and the pursuit of happiness. It's that equilibrium we are looking for. The black man is there with the change, and he is there, clear as day. He is in the map of life to help and guide me. There seems to be some chaos and confusion involved with him, and that is the riddle to fate I need to solve. Theja's skin is darker, and I sometimes think he is the dark man.

I read and Googled so much and found that I have a Mangli line in my palm, sometimes called Mangalik Dosh but only in the right hand. On my other hand, there is no Mangli line. I was born with Mars only in Leo, where it is good. My Mars is in my heart where you have courage and loyalty to love. I read how to improve this phenomenon, and it involves some strange things like marrying someone with the same lines or has the same astrology as you. My lines mean I am living the Buddha path, which can be a lonely way of life. But I don't have anything wrong with my birth chart. Which means someone has been an influence. I noticed that both of my parents have that Mangli line in their hands.

Someone who has Mars in their chart, in relationships, this can cause some harsh effects—some victimizing effects. So I gave serious thought to marring a tree or clay urn to help with any trouble in my life. It is a regimen I found. It should take care of any mayhem in my life, and I should be free then. I know this sounds funny, but it will trick fate, and then the chaos will stop. No more accidents and then maybe happiness and true freedom.

I also read that the "Manglik Dosha" person can have Asperger's syndrome. These people, like I said, have a lot of Mars in their astrology charts, which makes them want to fight, bicker and over negotiate in their intimate relationships. They have problems in controlling their feelings of anger, depression, and anxiety. Manglik Dosha has difficulties with small talk and empathizing with others. This somehow was an important find to me because I think it sort of explains something about myself and the man I attract. I'm still working through this one.

However, I downloaded so much and did not realize at the time that I was downloading a map about how to enlighten yourself. But it explains what you can expect with your enlightenment. You become so focused on improvement in all realms of life. You look for the perfection in life. I started to exercise my whole body and made a huge transformation. I even exercised my face. I started to clear my chakras. I became so focused on improvement on all areas in my life that I had forgotten about. I even worked on all my relationships, friends, mother, father, brothers, daughter, ex partner, coworkers; yes, even my pet. Everything became important to me. I even began to see things from the other person's perspective, like Gerry, and I learned so very much about men.

I was too hard on him; I don't know anything about his life. He didn't open up to me about anything. I only know that Gerry does not believe in God. He is still in question about that, I think. This plays an important role in a soul mate relationship. He also has a lot to think about when it comes to his children and wife. I don't even know if she works or what is going on there. I'm sure he wants to take care of all of them, and he feels this great burden to do so. So I was able to forgive him, and in that, I was able to release him. We are only friends now, and that is all

I started a new beginning, and I had to put the past behind me, which means I needed to forgive. Not just people in my life, but I needed to forgive myself for putting myself last and forgetting about that child inside wanting a hug, waiting so long for her "turn." The sobbing one, the hungry one, the thirsty soul; I felt bad for what I did to her. Now, I had to take care of her and nurture her needs even if they seem so insignificant, and I wasn't allowed to feel bad about doing it either. This was going to be hard. I had to start with just the small ones first. Like getting myself out there and making friends, find where I belong, so I can feel comfortable. I needed to discover myself. Even if I looked awkward stumbling around, trying to find my place even if it meant I had to allow myself to be vulnerable and take risk after all I am waking up!

I needed to draw the sword out of the stone, have courage to take a risk to really fall in love even if it was frightening because a great love can be that—both frightening and maddening with these incredible odds. I still love him and know Theja is the one I could love till the next lifetime and the next life. He is the perfect man for me.

Going through this experience of enlightenment has helped me to see and understand all the unexplained, secrets, and ideas. People can go crazy if they don't have the support they need while going through this experience. Luckily, I had my Indian guide, Theja, so thank you, Theja. But he really never told me what to do. He was just there every day in my e-mail with a kind word or two. His praising words meant everything to me. He has been a true friend, and good friends are hard to come by, and I can hardly wait to meet him, again in the flesh. He could be the love of my life, and I asked God for that. But I was ready for this experience to happen, and it was my fate. I remember tearfully crying out to God. Tears were the physical element to the creation. Along with my heart opening up to God for healing, my soul called to him. It was a deep, heart-wrenching emotion, and Theja felt this.

I did go to a professional psychic here in Saint Louis, Missouri. Her name is Rhonda K. Leifheit. She did a "Crossing of Paths" reading, and in that reading, I learned that Theja and I have lived many lives together, but two stood out as the most significant. Theja doesn't want to know about the lives before and for good reason. I know what happen, but the stories are very touching. My mother says that they are another story to be written.

I did have a life in India. I was a young woman there with much devotion to her spiritual path, but I was not one that took the vows of chastity, but that's all I will tell you. The other significant one was in the south of France. Again, I was devoted to a spiritual path and lived and worked in a convent, but again, I did not take any vows. This would explain what I was downloading, but in each of these lives, I had a purpose, and it was with Theja, and that will explain the intense devotion we share for each other today.

I have to keep one thing in mind, and that would be that these lives are in the past, and I may look back on them to learn something, but they are in the past, and I must live in the present one now.

If you ever get to see my story made on Facebook, that was done in 2010. You will see I had downloaded these past lives, and Theja recognized the story. I had no idea what I was doing at the time, but it felt right, and I did it with earnest purpose.

So this sums up my journey to self, and I'm learning about my intuition or that full-brain knowledge. I'm learning about empathics, and I know I am one. I am a quiet soul that can cry while reading a poem, and I love listening to music that moves me to dance or tears. I feel other people's pain, fear, joy, and love. I enjoy lying down in the grass on a blanket and looking at the stars. I marvel at the wonder of nature! I watch the sunset or sunrise. I feel like I am something of that creation and that emotion because there was so much love into making nature, by God.

I'm also studying more about soul mates and twin flames. I have to tell you that every sense I connected to Theja, my blood pressure changed, and I have always had low blood pressure all my life, but now it is textbook, and I'm a healthy women. I have proof of it at the doctors. The nurse once told me that I have the blood pressure of a young woman.

I've only just begun—my journey, and I'm making friends now with people in this area of work. I hope I was of some help to anyone going through the same experience. I don't claim to know more than anyone else out there. I just wrote the story to tell you what had happen to me. And if it helps you, then I feel good about that.

My life at this time was not making any sense, but I'm seeing the future in a more positive light. I know I will write more, and I plan to take more classes. The possibilities are endless to what I could do in my life, and I'm starting to see that. I know and trust that this story will reach those that need to read it because it is designed to happen in that way. I want to help those with the color purple added into their lives, and I'm sure some are children, or young adults as well as grown adults.

This story continues, and I have even more to write about because in the next book, I have more questions and answers. The story just keeps getting better.

Good luck on your journey and truly enjoy the "Entire Universe Experience." It's so wonderful! It's the lighting of a tree at Christmas. It's Buddha realizing he is the miracle. It's meaning is found in so much. I feel so very lucky to have been in the right place at the right time. This was my fate to write about the Universe and all its glory!

Acknowledgments

Thank you Lily for your patience and all those hours alone while I wrote and researched for this book. You are the reason why I try so hard in this life, and I hope I gain your trust in me again. I love you . . .

Mom and Dad, thanks for being wonderful parents. I couldn't have had it better, and thanks to my brothers and all my family!

Theja, for being my soul mate! Thanks for your kind, thoughtful patience and gentle guidance.

Linda Partridge, my sociology professor, who has given years of support on my behalf.

Mrs. Engelhardt thanks for being a trusted friend and for your helpful input.

Linda Roberts, my tarot card reader, thank you for your help.

Jenna and Norah, my astrologers, thanks for your guidance. It was a good thing I could trust you in my e-mail. You did help me so much! It was like God sent you . . .

Thanks to God, and Mother Earth, and all the Angels of Light . . . and the *Universe*.

Research

Indigo Childern:
www.namastecafe.com/evolution/indigo/whoarethey.htm

What is Tantra or Tantric:
www.beliefnet.com/Faiths/Buddhism/2000/09/what-Is-Tantra-Anyway.aspx

Kundalini:
www.wikipedia.org/wiki/Kundalini_syndrome

Soul-Mate and Twin Flame
www.enlightenspirit.com/enlightenspirit/soulmate.html

Domain and Range of a Function
www.analyzemath.com/DomainRange/DomainRange.html

Golden Ratio
www.mathsisfun.com/numbers/golden-ratio

Astrological Transits
www.wikipedia.org/wiki/Astrological_transit

Mangalik Dosh
www.jyotisha.00it.com/Manglik.com

Osho on Psychic Mediumship
www.messagefrommasters.com/Psychic-world/Psychic-Mediumship.com

Esoteric Training
http://bonniewells.com/esoteric_training

Index

A

Adams, Bryan, 47-48
  "Please Forgive Me," 48
ADD (attention deficit disorder), 66
ADHD (attention deficit/hyperactivity disorder), 21
American Constitution, 48
Anne, 13
appetite, 88-89
Asperger's syndrome, 92
astrologers, 86

B

Barb (Uncle Tom's wife), 18
Bertha (grandmother), 19
Betty (aunt), 33
Bruce (brother), 15-16, 21-22, 26
Buddha, 74, 77, 96
Buddha path, 81, 92

C

chaos, 88-89
Chet (grandfather), 18-20
Cindy (horse), 26
Cinnamon (horse), 26
coma, 57
courage, 88-89
Crossing of Paths, 94

D

Declaration of Independence, 48
déjà vu, 86
discouragement, 32

E

enlightenment, 72, 81, 91, 93-94
esoteric training, 85

F

Francis (grandfather), 29-31

G
Galileo, 13
Ganesha (Hindu god), 74
Gerry (Nancy's ex-lover), 36-38, 50-54, 89
golden ratio, 73, 81
Groundhog Day, 86

H
Hachiko, 39
Hanuman (Hindu god), 74
horses, analogies of, 88
Hyderabad, 75-76

I
Indian in the Cupboard, 39
intuitive gifts, 62, 90

J
Ji, 49
Jo, 13
Joann (mother), 14-17, 20-23, 25-26, 28-29, 34, 53

K
karma, 80, 86
Keller, Helen, 88
Kundalini, 72

L
Lamaze, 64
Leeuwenhoek, Antonie van, 13
Leifheit, Rhonda K., 94
Lily, 62-64, 66-67, 90-91, 97
Lincoln, Abraham, 13, 92
Little House on the Prairie, 25
"Little Red Riding Hood," 18

M
Mangalik Dosh/Mangli line, 92
Maria (Rodolfo's ex-wife), 57, 63
Mother Teresa, 48
Mrs. Shots (teacher), 28

N
Nina (sister-in-law), 59
Nixon, Richard, 32
Nosy (horse), 25-26, 28-29

O
ocean, 24, 63

P
patience, 54
peg leg, 31
Phantom of the Opera, 39
Plato (philosopher), 88
Platonic love, 88
"Please Forgive Me" (Adams), 48
pleasures, levels of, 88
"Process of Being," 35
profanity, 32-34
psychic mediumships, 72

R
Rascal (horse), 25-26
reason, 88-89
Remember Me, 39
retrograde motion, 86
Rodolfo (husband), 5, 55-63, 66, 90
Ruth (grandmother), 17, 31-32

S

Saagara Sangamam, 72
saddle, western, 29
Sea Biscuit, 39
sex, 51-52, 88
Shawn (brother), 15-16, 21-22, 26-27
shit, 32-34
Shiva (Hindu god), 74
Smokey (horse), 26
spirit, 88

T

tantra, 80-81
tears, 94
Theja (Indian friend), 48-50, 68, 72, 87
Tirupathi, 77, 79
Tom (father), 22-24
Tom (uncle), 17-18

V

VanHook, Nancy Jo
  accident of mother, 26-29, 88-89
  going to India, 73-80, 82
  relationship with brothers, 14-16
  relationship with daughter Lily, 65-66
  relationship with Gerry, 36-38, 50-54
  relationship with Rodolfo, 56-63
  relationship with Theja, 69-72, 81-82, 91
  using Facebook, 38-39, 48-49, 73, 95
Venkateswara (Hindu god), 74, 79

Y

yin and yang, 71

Edwards Brothers Malloy
Thorofare, NJ USA
May 29, 2013